Flash

Platform Studies
Nick Montfort and Ian Bogost, editors

Flash

Building the Interactive Web

Anastasia Salter and John Murray

The MIT Press   Cambridge, Massachusetts   London, England

MIT Press books may be purchased at special quantity discounts for business or sales promotional use. For information, please email special_sales@mitpress.mit.edu.

This book was set in Filosofia by Toppan Best-set Premedia Limited, Hong Kong. Printed and bound in the United States of America.

Library of Congress Cataloging-in-Publication Data

Salter, Anastasia, 1984–
Flash: building the interactive web / Anastasia Salter and John Murray.
    pages   cm. — (Platform studies)
Includes bibliographical references and index.
ISBN 978-0-262-02802-8 (hardcover: alk. paper) 1. Flash (Computer file) 2. World Wide Web.
3. Multimedia communications—Computer programs. I. Murray, John, 1986– II. Title.
TK5105.8885.F59S35 2014
006.7'8—dc23
                                        2014003874

10 9 8 7 6 5 4 3 2 1

Contents

Series Foreword

How can someone create a breakthrough game for a mobile phone or a compelling work of art for an immersive 3D environment without understanding that the mobile phone and the 3D environment are different sorts of computing platforms? The best artists, writers, programmers, and designers are well aware of how certain platforms facilitate certain types of computational expression and innovation. Likewise, computer science and engineering has long considered how underlying computing systems can be analyzed and improved. As important as scientific and engineering approaches are, and as significant as work by creative artists has been, there is also much to be learned from the sustained, intensive, humanistic study of digital media. We believe it is time for humanists to seriously consider the lowest level of computing systems, to understand their relationship to culture and creativity.

The Platform Studies book series has been established to promote the investigation of underlying computing systems and how they enable, constrain, shape, and support the creative work that is done on them. The series investigates the foundations of digital media—the computing systems, both hardware and software, that developers and users depend upon for artistic, literary, and gaming development. Books in the series will certainly vary in their approaches, but they will all also share certain features:

• A focus on a single platform or a closely related family of platforms.

• Technical rigor and in-depth investigation of how computing technologies work.

• An awareness of and discussion of how computing platforms exist in a context of culture and society, being developed based on cultural concepts and then contributing to culture in a variety of ways—for instance, by affecting how people perceive computing.

Acknowledgments

Special thanks to Adobe and the Flash developer community, whose incredible documentation and resources make studying a platform of this magnitude even possible.

This book exists thanks to Nick Montfort and Ian Bogost, editors of the Platform Studies series, and our editor Doug Sery. We benefited from the stories and insight of many people who've worked with and on Flash throughout the years, including Jonathan Gay, Jason Nelson, Stuart Moulthrop, Jason Scott, Arno Gourdol and Carlos Ulloa. Our colleagues and mentors at the University of Baltimore, University of California Santa Cruz, University of Maryland, Georgetown University, and beyond have all provided inspiration and support throughout this project: to name only a few, thanks to Noah Wardrip-Fruin, Michael Mateas, Matthew Kirschenbaum, Bridget Blodgett, Kathryn Summers, Deb Kohl, Aaron Reed, Jacob Garbe, Duncan Bowsman, and Jim Whitehead.

Screenshots throughout appear thanks to the generosity of their owners:

Figure 2.1: *Lil' Pimp*, feature-length Flash production, 2005, Mark Brooks

Figure 2.2: *Breakup Girl*, 1999, Lynn Harris and Chris Kalb

Figure 4.1: *Alien Hominid*, 2002, Tom Fulp

Figure 4.2: *Pico's School*, 2006, Tom Fulp

Figure 5.1: *I wish I were the Moon*, 2008, Daniel Benmergui

Figure 5.2: *Pax*, 2003, Stuart Moulthrop

Figure 5.3: *The Company of Myself*, 2009, Eli Piilonen

Figure 7.1: *Phone Story*, 2011, Paolo Pedercini

Introduction

The cover of the 2006 *Time* magazine "Person of the Year" issue featured a glossy, reflective image of a personal computer screen with the controls of a web video at the bottom of a monitor under the bold-faced word: "You." A provocative headline below reinforced the message: "Yes, you. You control the Information Age. Welcome to your world." The article proclaimed the reliance of the web on a broad population of content makers motivated by passion while "working for nothing and beating the pros at their own game" (Grossman 2006). According to *Time*, we'd entered the era of the LOLcat and "i can haz cheezburger"; the age of the YouTube dance sensation and the amateur music video parody; the year of the blogger and the Wikipedia editor. This "Information Age" brought with it web 2.0 and heightened expectations of interactivity from web-based media. Clay Shirky observed that these new activities were this generation's outlet for a cognitive surplus of incredible collective power: a surplus of mental energy once reserved for the consumption of television or gin but now turned toward production (Shirky 2011). With this revolution came new attention to amateur works and the apparent overthrow of traditional models of publishing, thanks in part to new accessible distribution channels. This new web appeared to be inherently democratic, with every voice given an equal opportunity to reach a broad audience; however, any such equality of entry is an illusion, and even the apparent ease of access owes more to the platforms shaping the web than anything inherent in the network. *Time* credited networks such as YouTube and Facebook with providing the tools of this revolution, but ignored the underlying technologies that empowered amateur creation—and the role those platforms played in determining what types of content would be the stickiest and easiest to create by newcomers.

As traditionally defined, a platform is a foundation from which ideas and ideologies are launched. In software studies, Ian Bogost and Nick Montfort define a platform as a hardware or software system that provides the "foundation of computational expression" (Montfort and Bogost 2009). Some platforms appear self-contained: a Nintendo game console, for instance, has a set configuration and manufacturer whose particular rules govern the system's potential. Personal computers vary more wildly in their capabilities thanks to the amalgamation of hardware and the range of operating system choices and software that extend their core functionality. Those capabilities might be termed "affordances"—a term used by Donald Norman to describe the "actual" and "perceived" properties of a thing, whether that thing is a piece of hardware or software or simply a pencil (Norman 1988). This term, which can be used in many ways, is helpful in examining platforms as foundations that offer certain possibilities and in doing so shape the creative works they underlie. Affordances are not just properties of a platform: they become suggestions and frameworks for the works built upon them. When examining the web (and particularly the participatory, "you"-driven web 2.0), a number of different platforms and affordances are at work that are impossible to isolate—and their various affordances have fundamentally shaped the web as a space of discourse, creativity, and interactivity.

The web itself—web 1.0, to some—relies on an agreed language foundation, HTML, for its structure. HTML, or HyperText Markup Language, was first released in 1991 by Tim Berners-Lee as part of the architecture of the World Wide Web (Berners-Lee 1994). That initial set of markup has morphed and evolved over the years as new versions and standardizations of key features made their way into the growing number of web browsers. Classic HTML was static as far as the user was concerned: its affordances were minimal, and early websites reflected strong restrictions on content types that corresponded with low bandwidth on early dial-up connections. Instead of the modern capabilities that rival desktop applications, early HTML provided a means to link files: the hyperlink offers a way either to move between documents on the web or between nodes within a page. When combined with other web technologies, HTML acts as both a skeleton and a lingua franca for more sophisticated display of content. The addition of CSS, or cascading style sheets, separates format from the structure provided by HTML. HTML originally mixed the two, including the infamous blink tag as other tags evolved haphazardly through differing support by browsers, before the expectations of web content demanded formatting and structure well beyond those foundational capabilities. Adding interactivity beyond a link-based graph structure was more complicated; it required using additional scripting languages, or different integrated web platforms, to interpret and make the content responsive.

Among this tangled web of platforms, one stands out as a driving force of the "you" revolution and web interactivity. An Internet user loading up YouTube or an online game in 2006 would likely be launching Adobe Flash Player, one of the options for adding self-contained multimedia or interactive content to a website. Adobe Flash Player is a browser extension that offered a browser-based environment with affordances well beyond the traditional web, extending the palette of online content capabilities dramatically over the years. Users of Flash Player might not even notice their reliance on Flash as, once installed, it became a fairly seamless part of the browsing experience. Flash is a multimedia platform that started as a simple animation package and grew to offer an incredible range of opportunities to author media experiences on the web. Gaming magazine *Edge* pointed out that Flash and the communities it inspired were at the real forefront of participatory culture, even if sites like YouTube were getting all the credit (Edge Staff 2007). Flash game developers cite the platform's accessibility and ease of quick prototyping for artists and the friendliness of its design that allows amateur creators to experiment. In 2005, just before *Time* announced the year of the amateur content creator, Lev Manovich declared that "Generation Flash" had emerged: a new class of media artists that "writes its own software code to create their own cultural systems, instead of using samples of commercial media" (Manovich 2005). He noted that this generation did not necessarily have to use Flash to be part of this movement, but were instead characterized by what he considered "Flash aesthetics": a style that could be translated to Shockwave, DHTML, Quicktime, and many other competing platforms for web multimedia. These other tools have some of the capabilities of Flash: animation, games, and dynamic, responsive web sites. These qualities are not exclusively the domain of Flash. But Flash's contributions, especially as a unified platform, set expectations for web content so high that the name of the platform is embedded in the aesthetic, and Manovich's generation of content-creators and artistic innovators could be rightly labeled as products of the Flash platform—a platform that itself emerged ten years before his writing, and with a very different set of affordances. This convergence of people and platform recalls Marshall McLuhan's often quoted (and often misused) concept: "the medium is the message" (McLuhan

1964). As McLuhan unpacks the concept, "This is merely to say that the personal social consequences of any medium—that is, of any extension of ourselves—result from the new scale that is introduced into our affairs by each extension of ourselves, or by any new technology." Generation Flash is a prime representation of this consequence of extension. The scale of self-amplification and creation that Flash enables likewise amplified the web.

Positioning Flash: A Brief History

Flash began its life as "SmartSketch," a software program that evolved from a tablet drawing program into an animation tool. The program's evolution reflected the search for the problem that Flash was solving: the delivery of dynamic content, not just static pages, over the web. In our interview in 2012, Flash creator Jonathan Gay recounts how the project evolved (see the appendix):

> The main constraint was our time and not understanding what the problem was. Do we put sound in the first version, what kind of features? Initially we built a drawing package that influenced a lot of things, but wasn't a product for the Internet. And then we said, well, we have drawing, let's add animation to it. There weren't a ton of choices, it was more gradual: How do we build it, what do we put in it next? What's the most important thing: what do we build next?

After retooling and refocusing its efforts for web-based distribution, FutureWave Software released FutureSplash Animator on August 19, 1996. Among its high-profile initial clients were Disney and Microsoft, both choosing FutureSplash for its ability to deliver TV-like graphics with small file sizes (Allbusiness.com 1996) for their respective web launches. After four years and a $500,000 investment by its founders, FutureWave was acquired by Macromedia only a few months after the release in December 1996, bringing it to the attention of the wider technical market. With this came the change of the product name that shortened the wordy title to Macromedia Flash 1.0.

The packaging of FutureSplash proclaimed it "a complete web site graphics tool," emphasizing the origins of SmartSketch and not yet acknowledging how the product would come to dominate its bigger brothers. The slogan suggested limitations to animated banner ads and a snazzier version of the "Under Construction" images that were everywhere on the young web as virtual homesteaders figured out how to colonize the media space. The purchase by Macromedia added additional complexity to FutureSplash's identity, as Macromedia Director 5's inclusion of an option to export to Shockwave, a format similar to Flash, made it a viable platform for creating web-based animation and interaction. Director had a long history as a multimedia editing platform, starting out as MacroMind "VideoWorks" with very limited graphic capabilities in the 1980s. Macro-Mind's founder and leader up to the merger with Macromedia in 1991, Marc Canter, explained the vision that drove his software design: "Because we had a direct connection to the animators, designers and musicians who were using our tools, we knew exactly what features and capabilities they needed . . . One thing we knew—that the world needed end-user 'tools' that could be used by artists, musicians and designers—to create this 'stuff'—this combination of graphics, text, music and interactivity that we knew was possible" (Canter 2003). Director's capabilities, however, were formulated for delivery over CD-ROM, whereas Flash would flourish in its newfound home across the web.

At the time of Flash's acquisition by Macromedia, Director and Flash were competitors with more than a few similarities. Even so, Flash's early adaptations were in response to the needs of the web. Director's powerful capabilities translated into higher download times and a greater bulk in the Shockwave extension, while Flash was more limited but optimized. These optimizations built on key goals set by the team early on, giving Flash an edge in the race to play content. The creative metaphors of Flash and Director show a strong parallel, although Flash's did not extend nearly as far into the moviemaking aspects. After Macromedia was purchased by Adobe, Director stayed desktop-focused while Flash dominated web interactivity and animation. The existence of the two programs within the same ecosystem allowed them to capitalize on each other's design and affordances, to the point where Macromedia and Adobe would both have to clarify use cases for each given the substantial overlap between them. Eventually the ability to embed Flash content in Director further blurred the lines between the platforms.

The 1997 introduction of the Aftershock utility as part of Macromedia's "Universal Media" initiative addressed the technical limitations of authoring a single experience for multiple platforms. The Universal Media initiative described the core aspiration of both Flash and Java for a singular input, universal set of target formats: "With all of the available output alternatives, Director and Flash movies will now be able to be viewed by an unlimited audience" (Macromedia, Inc. 1997). This was also a preview of initiatives to making Flash accessible to non-coders: just as the first version of Flash involved no conception of objects or scripting, Aftershock allowed for the immediate embedding of a finished Flash project into an HTML document without the user understanding the internal construction of either. Aftershock offered a graphic interface for immediate export. Macromedia was clearly aiming at reaching a broader range of amateur creators, who wanted to distribute immediately over the web. This set the foundation for the future, as Canter noted in an interview in 2004: "The evolution of tools has brought us to the point where the entire business models are changing and the essence of what tools are has shifted from something a professional uses, to something everyone will need to know how to use . . . the content in our lives will get treated like content from Hollywood" (MacManus 2004). Such a tool might expedite the work of a professional user, although the limitations were many and included page layout, as seen in the interface. Instead, these interfaces targeted amateurs more familiar with file management systems than programming.

Each version of Flash extended the platform's capabilities and gradually integrated a scripting language alongside the animation framework of the timeline. The release of Flash 5 coincided with a big change in the authoring of Flash: ActionScript was now a programming language, and as such it could be attached to MovieClips, frames, and sprites. The syntax, or format and ordering of the language, also changed drastically. The language moved from the custom set of commands that are closer to the capabilities of the player to a more standardized language on which JavaScript is also based: ECMAScript. The slash syntax, which allowed authors to identify objects like a web address, remained in this version, as did the toolbox. Many programmers encountered Flash as a first programming environment after transitioning from the markup syntax of traditional web development. But Flash 5 was now recognizable even to developers bringing expectations from popular systems programming languages such as C or Java: a few key elements were adopted, including parameterized function calls and local variables that enabled higher-level organization of the code. These features enabled coders to reuse and organize their code. This was particularly relevant to games, which often share a great deal of functionality with other works in a genre. Flash 5 also included the first debugger, which allows programmers to see into the code's state as it runs. Along with these changes to the language, ActionScript was moved from a specific subeditor in the interface attached to MovieClips into its own file extension, ".as." This allowed programmers to use the same code in different projects and helps organize code based on functionality.

ActionScript's introduction, however, also marked an acceleration of complexity as well as an increase in power. First under Macromedia and increasingly under Adobe's ownership, the development of the platform moved away from the original intended purpose: a friendly authoring tool for not-quite-end users. Flash was instead split under market pressures between the needs of enterprise customers and the increasingly attractive mobile markets. The inexorable march of mobile would lead to Flash Lite, while the enterprise market birthed the Flex SDK, whose mission was to make creating relatively similar applications easier. While these tools leveraged the platform's virtual machine, the original runtime provided developers with a means to bypass the turbulent demands of web standards.

Flash was, for the better part of the 2000s, the de facto standard for dynamic online multimedia. Canter described the philosophy behind multimedia as a rejection of arbitrary categorizations in art: "We foresaw multimedia as a new art form to merge the medias together-so you could paint with the violin and make music with the paintbrush" (MacManus 2004). The platform's goals stayed consistent across owners and even through the expansion into enterprise and mobile. However, the accumulated difficulty in establishing a universal language for interactive and creative web experiences proved extraordinarily difficult. Other platforms tried to establish themselves as a universal, and some—including Java—offered similar portability but without the artist-friendly development environment that Flash featured. Flash was designed with professionals in mind, but it was co-opted by an amateur web, with users who in turn created resources and communities that steered the platform through experiments and creative works and into the current expectations for what multimedia experiences delivered on the web are capable of. As Flash's influence has spilled out beyond the browser window, we can see the consequences of the platform's styles and drawing tools everywhere from Cartoon Network to iPad games.

In our examination of Flash's impact, we will be considering Flash as both a platform for developing and for distributing content. Flash refers primarily to Flash Player, which interprets the ".swf" (hereafter SWF, which originally stood for "Shockwave Flash" format but eventually was generalized to "Small Web Format") file type. Most of those files are built using the primary Flash development environment, which has changed dramatically over the years as first Macromedia and later Adobe repackaged and extended its affordances. The SWF file format packages the vector graphics, timeline animation, and compiled ActionScript created within the development environment for interpretation within the browser. "Compiling" code involves transforming source code into something a machine can read. Flash compiles into an intermediate format in a similar way to Java, where a virtual machine interprets the code. The files are designed to be compressed and delivered through the web, so they are difficult to reverse-engineer once compiled. However, Flash Player can also interpret SWF files created by tools other than official Flash development tools, and these too must be understood as part of the platform's ecosystem. The consumer of Flash content sees only the playable material in the browser, regardless of how it was compiled.

Flash as Platform

The year of "You" also happened to be Flash's tenth anniversary, and while Flash itself didn't warrant a mention in that issue of *Time*, many of the networks mentioned—including YouTube—relied exclusively on Flash. Flash's tenth anniversary was celebrated around the web by a community of creators who had seen it evolve from a limited vector animation tool to a fully featured web platform and played a role in shaping that evolution: "Flash is, and always has been, a direct incarnation of what web designers and developers have requested over the years. Macromedia didn't believe in locking a lab full of software engineers away and leaving them to their own devices to improve the product. Instead, they went directly to the people who use the product, and asked them what they wanted. This is still the case today" (Voerman 2006). Flash creators further expressed their love of the platform through their own creative works. The "Nectarine" team released a tenth anniversary animation showing Flash as an evolving superhero for the web, gaining new skills and changing his costume with each release until his 2006 high-performance incarnation. The clean lines and shapes of the animation itself reflected the style that Manovich associated with Flash aesthetics: a style that had over the course of a decade become instantly recognizable.

Those same Flash aesthetics provoke strong opinions: user-experience designer Jakob Nielsen (2000) wrote that Flash was "99% bad" thanks to its almost excessive support for dynamism that encouraged bad design, "gratuitous animation," and the abandonment of information hierarchy in favor of flashiness. Nielsen is criticizing design decisions that can be made using any platform for web development, but singling out Flash as a culprit. This is Flash's scale: the go-to technology of the active and interactive web, responsible for aesthetics both loved and hated. Likewise, those who love Flash have formed loud and active communities sharing new ideas and celebrating experiments, as Flash developer Stacey Mulcahy explained at Flash's tenth anniversary:

Flash has taught me about the importance of resourcefulness and community as a developer. The Flash community is a vibrant and open one, because the members make an effort to give back to the community as much as they have taken from it over the years. Getting help in the Flash community is often just a forum or blog posting away. People are constantly posting experiments or insights that push the boundaries of the technology. It's hard not to be inspired. (Mulcahy 2006)

Flash's popularity as an entry point for beginning programmers, along with this accessible community of knowledge, was vital to its adoption as a near-universal authoring environment for the web. In 2009, Adobe released a survey that suggested Flash was king of Internet multimedia, reaching 99 percent of Internet viewers as opposed to Java's 81 percent (Millward Brown 2009). Adobe declared Flash to be a "pervasive software platform," powered by its community of users and the "2 million professionals" then estimated to be developing content for its player (Millward Brown 2009). We will consider both the user Flash seemed to cater to in features, design, and marketing and the real users who in turn shaped Flash to their needs. Flash, unlike fixed hardware platforms, could adapt to perceived opportunities, reflecting an uncertain development context despite constant growth. The emotional charge the popular platform inspired in its creators was as powerful as the pragmatic and ideological attacks it sustained. The platform's aspirations led it to become increasingly fragmented in its focus, attempting to please users despite disjoint and often conflicting needs. Our approach reflects this multilayered platform's depth and pervasiveness; separating where possible technological limitations from the economic and social forces shaping the platform's evolution with attention to both the development and deployment of content.

Previous volumes of the Platform Studies series have primarily addressed hardware: the Atari Video Computer System, the Nintendo Wii game console, and the Commodore Amiga personal computer. These examples have the advantage of being grounded in finite hardware systems, often with relatively consistent setups and affordances determined by one development group. Flash depends on hardware, but is far from integrated with any particular hardware configuration. Thus, unlike previous titles in the Platform Studies series, our study of Flash will look at how a software platform subsists between creators and their audience, shaping a user's relationship with computer hardware by enabling certain experiences on it and attempting (and often failing) to facilitate others. As Ian Bogost and

Nick Montfort, the series editors, explain it, platform studies is concerned with investigating the connections between hardware, software, and creative works. Flash, consisting mostly of virtualized hardware, is inherently more generalized in its hardware needs. As a software platform, Flash exists in a more abstract space than consoles or personal computers. Unlike hardware, where each iteration is at least in technical specifications a fairly clear progression from the previous generation, Flash's iterations are not necessarily straightforward improvements. Matthew Fuller points out that this is common in software development, which is "not subject to the rigor of the requirement for the 'better and better'" (Fuller 2006). While Fuller defines this trait in regards to software that is not aimed at consumers, the same can be said of any software: "better and better" is difficult to define without clear benchmarks. Flash has evolved repeatedly and often haphazardly through its eleven runtimes, two virtual machines, and four programming languages. Its constant expansion of scope was as much in response to developer desire as it was to rising expectations from end users and stakeholders. In our interview, Gay noted how critical developers were in shaping the platform's early direction:

It was a gradual realization. There are different ways to define platform. Macromedia acquired Flash pretty early on; we were sitting as the little kid next to Director hoping not to get canceled. It was a gradual realization: "Wow, they have this developer community. This is an amazing thing. You have these people who have all these mental structures about how to use your tool. And the things they do inspire other people and there's this positive feedback loop. And they make money building this stuff." To me, that's the key part of the platform: when you have this community around it, and they are doing things, and they are adding value on top of it, they become invested in it. We saw it in developers first, and "Wow, it looks as if Flash is doing that, too."

Because the Flash platform has been primarily web-based, its reach extended to a wider range of users and thus played a pivotal role in defining gaming outside of dedicated platforms. Our approach will contribute insights into how such web-based platforms innovate through and despite translations onto successive hardware platforms. In particular, we'll consider the feedback loop established by its continually changing capabilities and how its identity in popular culture came about as a direct result of the developers building for the platform rather than those whose jobs were to build the platform. This book positions Flash as both a creative platform and a communal platform. It is not inherently social in the way that the Nintendo Wii is (as addressed by Steven Jones and George Thiruvathukal in their work on that platform), but it is designed as a tool for sharing (Jones and Thiruvathukal 2012). As the processing power and capabilities of personal computers have grown, Flash's own capabilities have correspondingly expanded, sometimes to its detriment, as in the case of the rapid growth of smartphone usage with their more limited hardware. Thus our attempt to capture Flash within these pages is subject to our acceptance of it as a platform constantly in flux, adapting to the changing environment created by hardware, software, and its own users.

Bogost and Montfort suggest there are five traditional layers of study common in our typical approach to media: reception, interface, form/function, code, and platform. The platform is "the abstraction beneath the code," whose construction permeates all levels of influence (Montfort and Bogost 2009). Demarcating the boundaries of the platform is difficult where software is concerned. Software itself transcends code and interface: Manovich defines software as "a layer that permeates all areas of contemporary societies" (Manovich 2013, 15). As a software platform of incredible range and influence, Flash has absolutely permeated through our culture and media, both through its stronghold on the computers it was designed for and in its aesthetic legacy and the altered expectations that resulted from it. Likewise the underlying structures and decisions made at the lowest levels have had a definitive influence on the evolution of content created using it. We'll consider both the layers of Flash as it evolved in abstraction and code serving a function, and the positioning of Flash works and user-developers—the reception and interface area of analysis typical to media studies.

When we talk about Flash, we're talking about an ecosystem of software: the many incarnations of the Flash development environment, the different versions of the Flash Player, the related specifications and the bytecode produced by the Flash compiler and interpreted by the various players. The Flash development environment bridges hardware and operating systems—primarily Mac OS and Windows PC—while the player has steadily targeted additional platforms as they came out. Simply documenting the Flash software ecosystem could fill a volume of this size, and we will not attempt to address this entire range. The full history of Flash is not well-documented, but it does live on in seemingly endless volumes of instructional books dedicated to each iteration of the environment with examples and best practices. We will be pulling from this rich history to assist in identifying the key aspects of the platform, including the instrumental Flash development environment and the application programming interfaces. The philosophy represented by the development environment and the consequences of the key abstractions and metaphors realized by the Flash API permeate the Flash platform, echoing throughout the Flash ecosystem and beyond.

Using the lenses of media studies, critical code, and software studies, we will examine Flash's contribution to the landscape of online media and its role in defining web genres, including "Flashimation," browser-based gaming, and Internet-enhanced applications. Unraveling Flash's history and the role of competing interests of performance, security, developers and users also offers insight into the fate of the next universal languages that hope to supersede its relevance. User-developer involvement historically took place across periodicals, forums, wikis, and newsgroups, which is unique to a platform existent in this period of the web. Consequentially, that is where the focus of our assessment of decision and responses between the communities can glean the most insight. Flash's evolution is particularly useful in understanding the transformations inherent in any non-fixed platform. Its context moved from hypertext to web 2.0, from game arcade to social gaming's cornerstone and from web plug-in to Internet application operating system. Flash's dual role in the critical evolution of aesthetic and procedural affordances has shaped the participatory web and online multimedia, but the platform's ambiguous positioning in the field of openness and its defeat as a web extension in the garden of the iPhone ultimately prevented the platform from maintaining its status as a dominant standard, de facto or otherwise.

Our Approach

The platform studies series is traditionally based on collaboration, in part because of the diversity of disciplinary perspectives necessary to consider the different layers at which a platform exerts its influence. We are likewise from diverse backgrounds: one of us is in media studies and digital narratives, while the other is from computer science and game studies. We are both interested in Flash as a fundamental force that shaped how the web was perceived as well as Flash's role in enabling digital narratives and new forms of gaming. Both of us grew up with the web, making our own experiments in Flash and spending hours on Flash game sites and watching early hits like *Homestar Runner* make their way into popular culture. We have experienced Flash in several ways ourselves: as a development platform and as a tool for delivering content, as a space for artistic expression and a medium for play, as an instructional medium for teaching upcoming coders to create interactive art, and as an apparently diminishing medium still informing the landscape of today's dynamic web. Flash is behind everything from web banner ads and portfolio sites to animation and gaming. Its versatility allows it to impact a range of media. But many of these resulting works render the platform almost invisible, as some users aren't even aware of their reliance on the Flash plug-in until it is blocked. This transparency makes Flash easy to overlook, a tendency that perhaps explains the absence of Flash as more than a technical footnote in the dominant history of media studies: while many tomes have been devoted to the use and application of Flash, none have examined Flash as an object of critical study.

Thus Flash has been noted by several disciplines but rarely studied, thanks in part to that same transparency that makes it an accepted and often unquestioned part of the web's framework. Media studies approaches to the web have often considered the communities and works that Flash makes possible, but not the platform itself, or its role in shaping the ecosystem that makes those communities and their productions possible. The last decade has seen a number of theorists examine the rise of "participatory culture," which Henry Jenkins describes as one in which everyone is active in creating and mediating the culture (Jenkins 1992). This correlates with the democratization of publishing across media, along with the aesthetic impact of this media landscape on more traditional media venues. Studies of participatory culture as part of media often end at the level of reception, or more rarely of interface, rather than delving into the underlying structures. We'll consider these top-level implications of Flash works, but our goal is to better understand the position of Flash as a platform for shaping the discourse of this online (r)evolution.

One of the greatest influences of Flash has been in the space of gaming, and thus Flash games and the emergence of virtual arcades is already part of the discourse of game studies. Game studies is highly interdisciplinary, though typically focused more on the playable object than on the software underneath it. This interface/reception focus is changing, and we will be drawing on the related disciplines of critical code and software studies to further illuminate Flash games and their role in continually pushing the boundaries of the platform's affordances. However, Flash projects are most often released in their compiled form, so we will be discussing both completed works and internal workings where we have been able to acquire the source: this limitation is always a problem when studying software.

Throughout the book, we will zero in on some of the technical elements of Flash that most illuminate the platform's affordances, as well as their context and role in defining the very nature of web interactivity. Flash is a proprietary product, despite the semantic war to position it one way or another. Its creators are inextricably bound to the interests of its owners, Adobe and Macromedia. This dynamic compounds an already complex ecosystem of software layers and competing technologies, but is vital to understanding the insights into the platform's legacy. User-developers are also responsible for creating many of the libraries and resources that are integrated with Flash as a platform, and they must therefore be considered alongside it as part of Flash's role in shaping scripting and procedural literacy in a broader context.

Flash is, however, primarily a platform for the creation and distribution of software. There are several lenses for considering the nature of software: software studies and critical code studies provide an important starting point. Early Flash did not require the manipulation of code as we would recognize it, while the primary language—ActionScript—developed more complexity over the years. Flash is inherently visual, and its code is often intertwined with images, movie clips, and objects in its editor. We will begin by examining those early visual works and delve into the layers of Flash's code—both as a software platform and a platform for the development and release of software. From these roots, we will consider the Flash platform as a force in the production of culture across mediums, returning to the concerns of media studies and the humanities. These many layers are inseparable, though they are often studied in isolation. We hope to bridge that gap in understanding software platforms.

The Book's Plan

It is impossible to address the full scale of Flash works. Many are released anonymously or pseudonymously, and communities dedicated to Flash each host thousands of games, animations, and other works. Thus, we will be using a case study model and looking at a few significant examples chosen for their suitability to illuminate Flash's affordances and the role those affordances have played in constructing our experience of web multimedia. Chapter 2 examines Flash's contributions as a platform for developing animation. In particular, the concept of the timeline and keyframing allowed for the manipulation of MovieClips and the development of new animated shows without the requirements of a studio support team. This gave rise to an entire aesthetic, "Flashimation," with consequences not only for the web but also for the commercial production of animation. We'll look at several examples of Flash animation and their reception as well as their position as a cultural force removed from traditional "gatekeepers" of commercial animation.

As Flash evolved, the demands of web developers and an increasingly dynamic model of the web brought new affordances for experience design. In chapter 3, we'll look at the evolution of the Flash platform for scripting and interactive design through the lens of platformers. Flash has been repeatedly used to recreate and extend Mario's adventures. These tutorials and their developers were part of the force behind the development of Flash web arcades and communities dedicated to Flash as a tool for digital distribution of immediately playable games. Many of these games are part of what Jesper Juul termed the "casual revolution," as they are inherently cross-platform with none of the demands of dedicated hardware or even dedicated installations that accompany most games. The type of gaming that Flash enabled resembles the casual gaming that Jones and Thiruvathakal (2012) describe in their platform study of the Wii. But while the Wii requires hardware and invades the living room, Flash brought casual gaming to nearly any computer, as a background escape in the office. In chapter 4, we'll examine some of the games and genres that emerged through Flash's role in reconstructing the browser as a games portal powered by many user- and developer-sustained communities.

The variety of affordances built in to Flash to accommodate three different development cases—interactive websites, animation and game design—were picked up by experimental creators who transformed and combined them to create new media art. In chapter 5, we'll look at different forms and genres of new media art, including electronic literature and art games, and the strong presence of Flash as a creative tool. There are two primary ways experimenters interacted with the platform: they either took the affordances of the platform and the expectations users brought to Flash works and subverted them in the production of art, or broke out of the affordances and created new systems for their art. We'll examine examples of both models and the implementation of several works, including Stuart Moulthrop's "textual instrument" *Pax* and Daniel Benmergui's wistful art game *I wish I were the Moon*.

While many of the examples under examination in this text clearly owe their existence to the openness and sharing model of Flash's developer community, Flash historically has had an uneasy relationship with openness. In chapter 6, we'll depart from examining a single media artifact to contextualize Flash's stance on openness and standards. A software platform that pervades the web must compete not only on the basis of performance and ease of use, but also in its relevance. Flash's owners systematically opened up parts of the platform in an attempt to maintain their control over the platform as well as the platform's value. Many of these choices reflected an awareness of the value of open source software, as well as the ongoing value that the owning company obtained from the control. The two strategies met in a platform-defining battle over the ability to participate in the success of Apple's own proprietary platforms.

Flash has recently been declared dead, and as of November 2011 Adobe acknowledged it was no longer pushing forward with Flash as a tool for mobile: Adobe noted that it had made a "long term commitment to Flash Player on desktops" but ceded mobile to HTML5 (Parr 2011). However, not only is Flash not dead, but its role as the definitive cross-platform tool for web-based experiences cannot easily be replaced. We'll look at Flash alongside HTML5, and consider the future of Flash—and its legacy—in chapter 7. Flash as we have known it may fade, but its influence continues to be felt on the web. Flash did not merely power the integration of interactive multimedia on the web, it defined it.

Introduction

The simplest task to complete in nearly any version of the Flash production software is the animation of a bouncing ball. The software's built-in vector graphics rely upon mathematical expressions to produce simple shapes rather than pixel-by-pixel images. This interface makes placing a simple ellipse quick and simple. Every Flash project includes a central canvas whose contents are governed by a timeline. Scrolling ahead on the timeline will show that same static circle awaiting action. Designating a new destination for the circle at a later point on the timeline will move it, and an algorithm fills in the space in the middle with an approximation of the ball's movement based on a chosen formula. The most important places of the ball are the "keyframes," which the animator designates: all of the intermediate positions are generated by the software. Animation in Flash is thus point-and-click for the user, but mathematical in nature. Flash's fundamental affordances stem from its original purpose as drawing tool that found purpose as a platform for animated web graphics. The evolution of the style that would be known as "flashimation" owes a great deal to the optimization of the processing of keyframes in the metaphor of Flash's timeline, which we will examine in this chapter. Flash's approach uses mathematical calculation instead of artists to fill in the spaces between keyframes. This fundamentally transforms the process of animation, representing the distinction Noah Wardrip-Fruin builds from Chris Crawford's comparison of data versus processing intensive labor

(Wardrip-Fruin 2009). Hand-drawn animation requires the creation of every cell individually, and the final project is the collection of all the data involved. Flash and other computer animations programs care only about data at certain key points on the image: the rest is filled in by processes that make the leap from image to image. Animating a complex or long work by hand requires a huge team to generate the data needed for every frame, while computer animation in Flash outsources much of the work to the computer hardware, allowing a single user to create complex animations. Managing the demands these processes place on both the user's computer and the server was key to the planning of Flash as a platform. In our interview (see the appendix), Jonathan Gay described how the needs of the simplest animation determined Flash's approach to loading assets and managing resources:

> The original inspiration was that we wanted to have an animation start playing before it was fully loaded. And we wanted it to be as small as possible, so using a dictionary approach where you have a set of assets, and it's almost a compiler as you generate the SWF, where it's figuring, "What frame do I need these assets on? Okay, I'm going to put this shape here, this font here and this sound here, and once it's there, I'll use it." It just evolved from that.
>
> One of the early animations was this goofy thing, we had this artist who had a seal and he was bouncing a ball. That was a big deal; it's like, could you make the seal start moving as quickly as possible? You want to look for the optimal solution. And so the optimal solution was just send the media you need for that frame and reuse it as often as you can.

The simple example of a seal bouncing a ball can be clearly divided into the keyframe metaphor: the motion of the graphic is mostly contained in the up-and-down movement of the ball between a starting position on the seal's nose and a final position at maximum height in the air. The animation inherently loops, which is a common approach in web graphics that often run upon loading a site and continue indefinitely.

Flash emerged as a platform for animation long before its developers incorporated interactivity, scripting, or any of the other characteristics we associate with later generations of Flash. As part of the "you"-powered online revolution, Flash animation would bring new opportunities for production and distribution to already-established professional animators while further empowering new breeds of amateurs and professionals. Flash launched with roots in the established history of animation and succeeded in pushing it forward to democratize the platform. The movement from data to process-intensive computer animation would change not only who could animate, but what they could animate and what kind of audience could see the work.

Animation Offline

The bloodshot eyes of a deranged and sharp-toothed Chihuahua pulse as he tackles his bulbously blue-nosed companion, shouting "You eediot!" before the TV cuts to a commercial. If you turned on Nickelodeon in 1991, you might have been bombarded by these surreally distorted, animated visages of a simple-minded cat and psychotic dog featured on *The Ren & Stimpy Show*. The show stood out at the time on a network officially aimed at children by offering a decided rejection of any educational agenda, preferring slapstick violence and toilet humor. It was also a change from the Saturday morning cartoon approach of most networks to animation at the time. This unrestrained, hand-drawn artistry from the show's creator, John Kricfalusi, was a glimpse of the future of animation in a world that would later embrace *South Park* and *Family Guy*, but at the time Nickelodeon was less impressed despite the show's good ratings. After refusing to air "Man's Best Friend," an episode where the dog Ren beat his owner "George Liquor" with a paddle after a strange sequence of failed obedience training, the executives grew weary of battling over content and dismissed Kricfalusi. The series continued with a new team, toned down and less controversial, for three more seasons as Kricfalusi watched from the sidelines.

This was not a surprising turn of events at the time because the idea of creator-owned cartoons was a rarity and executives dominated the creative process. Producing a hand-drawn cartoon such as *The Ren & Stimpy Show* required a team of dedicated animators both to create the key moments and to fill in all the stages in between. There was little Kricfalusi could do to continue the series following his own vision. However, Kricfalusi kept the rights to two characters from the series—the ultra-conservative "George Liquor" and his "Idiot Nephew." Nickelodeon had never liked them and was happy to remove them from *The Ren & Stimpy Show*. But where could he take these characters without running into more conflicts or fighting distributors over creative choices? It wouldn't be apparent for a few more years, but the World Wide Web was about to provide the ideal distribution network for creators with projects just like his. This shift and the combination of the power of Flash and the growing ubiquity of the web would transform the future of animation.

The tools for bringing animation to the web would emerge alongside an industry still wedded to paper and pencil. In 1996, hand-drawn animation still dominated U.S. television, with the rise of shows such as *Dexter's Laboratory*, *Hey Arnold!*, and *The Mighty Ducks*. Animation was reaching beyond the confines of the children's audience, with MTV featuring shows like *Beavis and Butthead Do America*. Disney's most recent princess, *Pocahontas*, featured hand-drawn animation in its 1995 theatrical release even as *Toy Story* became the first feature-length film in theaters made using only computer-generated images, winning a special Academy Award for the achievement. There was a clear gap between computer-generated animation of Pixar's variety, with three-dimensional figures and a focus on near-realism, and the hand-drawn animation still filling the Saturday morning cartoon roster. Experimental animation did exist, but was limited to music videos and to the festival or arthouse scene. Because independent producers of animation had no clear way to reach a larger audience, only a few—such as *Fritz the Cat*—gained further notoriety. For most, mainstream animation dominated perceptions of the medium. Other projects used physical materials and word of mouth, such as the infamous *Spirit of Christmas* short films made by Trey Parker and Matt Stone in 1992 using paper animation. These cartoons, distributed as video Christmas cards, would eventually bring Parker and Stone to the attention of Comedy Central and lead to *South Park*. Technologies were rising to bridge that gap, bringing computerized techniques to animation that more nearly resembled hand-drawn than computer-generated work. While most companies focused on studio uses of computer animation, an unimagined market was waiting in amateur users—potential creators in a new, web-based medium creating their own computer-rendered animation, or even thwarted creators of edgy projects like Kricfalusi's George Liquor.

While animation itself was beginning to undergo a transformation in the still distributor-dominated markets of television and film, the growing popularity of the web and the personal computer had fundamentally changed the home. Information networks and specifically hypertexts became the core of what we know now as the World Wide Web. Even though corporations were the predictable colonizers of this new space, individuals decided what the web should look like. Spaces like GeoCities, a "neighborhood" on the web founded in 1994 for creating a metaphorical home, brought "homepages" forward and began charting the personal expressive potential of the space. However, the multimedia potential within these spaces was still very limited, and the content available on a personal computer screen still looked very different from what was possible in other media such as the aforementioned film and television. Hypertext itself was founded on text primarily, with images as a secondary concern. Multimedia was a distant afterthought, still searching for standards and systems that could overcome the barriers of limited download speeds, which topped out at 14.4kbit/s. The demand for multimedia, however, often exceeded the capabilities to deliver it.

Flash on the Web

Flash's core features represented the legacy of the integration of animation into what had originally been a drawing tool. Illustrator and other programs already held a strong market share in dedicated drawing platforms, so Flash's distinctiveness needed to be found elsewhere. However, the original version of the program that had become Flash (a drawing tool for pen computers) continued with a novel approach to vector-based drawing tools at the heart of the original timeline animation software. These changes were born out of Gay's experience with PostScript and his frustration at the number of steps and the thought process necessary to create vector art. In a white paper released concurrently with the original site, Gay describes the limitations and his approach:

> The user model for editing shapes is very simple and maps very well onto the visual representation of a drawing. The user thinks of their drawing as being made up of lines and of filled areas. . . . The most significant thing about this new model is that anywhere lines touch or cross, they are automatically connected and if a new line is drawn directly on top of an old line, the new line replaces the old line instead of simply being drawn on top of it. Also, instead of showing the user the Bézier curve handles, the application transparently deals with managing the curve segments and lets the user edit them simply by grabbing a corner or a line anywhere and dragging it. (Gay 1996)

These user-oriented features allowed Flash to stand toe-to-toe with existing drawing tools, and with the addition of a timeline and means to interpolate images, it would become viable as a stand-alone platform for creating animation. Users could work with these vector-based tools and assemble an animation directly or import textures and images to move and distort. This hands-on model also offers a glimpse of the intended authors: the drag-and-drop manipulation hides many of the underlying algorithms at work during the creation process.

This simplification moved Flash far from the roots of computer animation, which had begun in the 1960s with Lee Harrison III creating one of the first motion capture rigs, called ANIMAC. Artists in both traditional and interactive roles were now beginning to realize the potential for an all-digital workflow. Instead of using software such as Toon Boom to reassemble scans of art, the use of graphics tablets (or digitizing tablets) began to become more and more widespread and standardized. Using a mouse to draw images intended for digital use has been compared to using a brick or soap bar. Tablets enable artists to bypass the time-consuming method of scanning and tracing traditionally produced drawings with the aid of a lightbox. Wacom tablets, with their stylus pens and touch-sensitive mechanisms, would become a leader in the industry when it came to replicating and replacing the traditional drawing surface.

Animation systems would evolve further into two different types of systems: those specified by programming and interactive keyframe systems (Sturman 1998). The latter was the most practical, and consisted of automatically creating intermediate frame between keyframes, known as "inbetweening" or just tweening. This pictorial model allowed the amateur user to see the results of their animation clearly and immediately, without the need for any understanding of how the spaces in between moments would be filled. The program does the extrapolation, while the user does the work of the master animator. Gay explained the decision to integrate the animation and the vector drawing technology in an interview:

> The avenues for distribution [of animation] were video tape, CD-ROMs and television. The barriers were all too high to sell much animation software in those channels. But at the same time, the Internet was just starting to gain momentum and we thought this growth would make distribution of content easy enough, thus creating an interesting market for animation software. We also realized that the limitations imposed by slow modems would mean that a simple animation tool would have a chance to compete with more sophisticated software. That led us to add animation to SmartSketch. (Simpson 2008)

Of particular note is Gay's assertion that the limitations of slow modems opened the doorway to Flash, as these same barriers would hinder Director and Shockwave's web influence and make Flash palatable to a range of audiences with limited bandwidth. This "interesting market" that Gay describes encompasses the range of potential hobbyists, including the obvious—students of animation and professional animators with side projects—but also a wider range of anyone with a passing interest in animation as an expressive form. Gay recognized the potential of software aimed at the amateur, as the range of digital professional tools for animation that emerged couldn't meet their needs. The same users discovering the power of the personal computer, with Microsoft's Windows 95 setting a standard for accessible interfaces powered by metaphors drawn clearly from the physical desktop into virtual space, could work with Flash's direct manipulation paradigm to create in a medium that previously demanded professional teams and resources. The first versions of Flash were designed with animation in mind: interaction with a user, including input and processing it, was mostly absent. But as FutureSplash became Flash, the focus shifted from web graphics to "web multimedia." With each version the underlying action model and player expanded thanks to the ambitious projects by users who pushed the capabilities of the system. These extreme projects drove the platform's procedural expressiveness, or what Noah-Wardrip-Fruin (2009) has termed the capacity for "expressive processing," shaping it into a medium for processing and interactivity.

At the heart of Flash's success and power lies its compelling use of metaphor: the adoption of the "frame" as a fundamental unit of a Flash movie, and the "stage" as the setting where "characters" would perform actions, were familiar and comfortable concepts that worked together to present an experience. Even the original idea of calling an invocation of an action on a character "telling" evoked the experience and dynamics of directing a play. The entire user interface is set up to resemble a set of filmstrips. The simple example of bouncing a ball is so readily realized because the timeline makes visible the change over time dynamics instead of abstracting it at the level of algorithmic process. Animation itself consists of change of an object over time, which in the data-intensive model of hand-drawn animation would translate into piles of physical pages, so it follows that you can define an animated sequence by its endpoints, and further you should be able to step forward and backward in time. The consequence of this new way of thinking about animation contributes to changing the logic of animation, as Lev Manovich describes: "The paradigm of a composition as a stack of separate visual elements as practiced in cel animation becomes the default way of working with all images in a software environment—regardless of their origin and final output media . . . a 'moving image' is now understood as a composite of layers of imagery—rather than as a still flat picture that only changes in time" (Manovich 2013). This concept is visible in the layering of Flash content and in the understanding of Flash's animated images as procedurally generated. Subtly, seductively, the concepts of procedures and programming began to find representations and embodiment in the interface, hinting at the possible movies that could take advantage of them.

But Flash's creators would see beyond this metaphor of film early on, and apply the same principles of interactivity underlying the hypertextual nature of the web to their expectations of production in Flash. Gay described the challenge of building games and other interactive experiences in early Flash: "At the outset, I didn't foresee the importance of interactivity in Flash. The animation engine in Flash was inspired by my experience with games, but I did not expect that we would have the programming resources to invest in building a good interactive engine" (Simpson 2008). Creating real interactivity alongside timeline animation still required significant effort with the limited palette of actions available in Flash 2 and 3. "One of the craziest Flash movies I remember was someone building a pinball game in Flash 2," Gay related in an interview. "The only interactivity in Flash 2 was the timeline, button objects and 'go to frame' actions so the author of this game added every possible ball position to the movie. After seeing that, I instantly knew that our users, using only these simple tools, were creative and stubborn enough to do amazing things" (Simpson 2008). These power users were the predecessors to the users who later versions of the Flash platform would treat as the core, as the metaphors of film would be sliced and reconfigured to accommodate these reinterpretations that viewed the timeline not as a linear outline but as an authoring system capable of creating vastly different media experiences. The challenge of this early Flash pinball game reveals the power of bringing a different perspective to animation: jumping between each position of the pinball requires deconstructing the elements of a movie into their smallest parts, only to rebuild them into something continually reconfigurable and responsive. In our interview, Gay explained the surprise of this state-based interactivity: "It was a state machine where they had a bunch of frames and tell targets, and if you click the button at the right time, then it would go branch off that. This person was insane. It was an artist that wanted a pinball machine. It was a little bit of logic and lots of states out there. Once I saw that, nothing surprised me." He went on to explain that this type of approach pushed toward the Flash platform's potential for something beyond animation: "Certainly the aspiration with Flash was to be general-purpose. Let's make it as general-purpose as we can. It was one of the early platforms to use vector graphics and user interfaces, so we were thinking, 'Let's leverage that'" to make a general purpose platform'" (see the appendix). In this case, the purpose the user envisioned would soon become one of the platform's fundamental affordances.

Competitors to the Flash platform often focused on the type of interactivity that Flash would quickly integrate into its own toolset. While

Disney embraced Flash for its web multimedia, Warner Bros. tried Togglethis: a platform with "interactive character technology" that tried to minimize user downloads by storing characters on the client side and downloading only new "scripts" for them to enact. As the cofounder, Marc Singer, explained in an interview, the medium demanded a unique approach: "There's no reason to have cartoons on the Internet like on the television . . . for me the question is when are you going to have interactive characters?" (Brown 1997). While this technology didn't thrive, the possibility of interactive characters and looking beyond the model of television would influence future developments in Flash, including its key role as the streaming media platform of choice for YouTube in 2005.

Flash's first debut after its rebranding from FutureSplash Animator was fundamentally pre-scripting: the technical constructions were governed by the timeline, and the primary affordances were the built-in tool for drawing. As Flash expanded, a larger development team was able to add interactivity that the original platform could perform only through the manipulation of expert users. Thus, the first influence of Flash was on web animation, to the point where the two would be synonymous for over a decade, and many users saw no reason to upgrade to later versions because early Flash so clearly met their needs as an animation tool without the distractions of the scripting-oriented toolset. Thus, the Flash platform's influence on development is never limited to its most recent version, and the affordances of the timeline and keyframe cannot be ignored as insignificant even though more recent iterations of Flash have often focused primarily on scripted solutions to animation. Three primary user groups rose through the platform's low-procedural literacy requirement and clear parallels to traditional animation production. (We will delve further into Flash's relationship with procedural literacy in the next chapter, as we move into Flash as a tool for interactive works.) The tool was immediately picked up by professional creators and animators who brought their personal projects to the platform—or who became professionals through their success with Flash as a tool for production and distribution. A combination of low investment and lack of accountability allowed these professionals to pursue content that would never win the approval of broadcasting agencies, thus helping dissociate the stigma of cartoons as for children only through the rise of alternative and edgy content—giving Kricfalusi's George Liquor a second life. The second group included amateur creators, often working alone or in pairs, who could now quickly reach mass audiences through their own sites or new content aggregators and user-generated content communities. And finally, some power users took the platform to extremes through projects that either mimicked the scale of traditional animation or started to hint at the more interactive productions that were Flash's future.

Flashimation and the Rebirth of George Liquor

On October 15, 1997, the first Flash cartoon was announced on alt.anima-tion.spumco with the big claim: "Spumco has just made history by intro-ducing the first animated series created exclusively for the World Wide Web. These are also the only cartoons being produced today that are 100% TAMPER-FREE . . . No network execs or censors looking over the creator's shoulder" (Worth 1997). The cartoon in question was *The Goddamn George Liquor Program*, launched by Kricfalusi. No longer content to wait for a studio to allow him to pursue his vision, Kricfalusi saw in Flash a creative potential beyond the simple animations its producers promised. George Liquor and his nephew could finally find a new home in these eight one-minute episodes. The first episode of *The Goddamn George Liquor Program*, entitled "Babysitting the Idiot," opens with a static credits sequence in a style not unlike that of *Ren & Stimpy*. The title itself emerges on the bars of a flag, while the rest of the credits use Flash's characteristic vector shapes.

The credits reveal a legacy of professional animation, listing a team of people behind the production including creator and director John K, but are notably shorter than professional hand-drawn animation and created without the normal team that would be required to fill in the space between the keyframes. The scene opens idyllically with a rising sun. Transitions between frames are minimal, and much of the animation is confined to expressions or bouncing back and forth, as with the two-frame motions of arms going up and down with tweens filling the distance in between. Music plays as a cheerful sun rises and greets a worm, only to see the worm eaten by the "early bird." A smoking dog emerges, perhaps in homage to the cigar dog treats of the network-banned episode of *Ren & Stimpy*, and promptly and graphically defecates on the lawn while reading the comics page. This leads to a sequence showing poop rising and going about its day (rather like the character of Mr. Hanky on South Park). In that sequence alone, the sensibilities of network executives would no doubt be offended.

George Liquor himself appears a few seconds later, announcing "Hello, I'm George Liquor, American" as the phrase "GEORGE LIQUOR AMERICAN" appears behind him in red, white, and blue. On Nickel-odeon, George's last name, "Liquor," was censored. He whistles "Yankee Doodle Dandy" as he heads into the chicken coop, passing by hens and roosters to awaken his idiot nephew, encouraging him into a basket rather like one would a pet. As he heads back inside, he admonishes, "Tune in next week, or you're dead meat in the desert." The animation ends with a mock message of sponsorship: "Brought to you by: YOUR AD HERE." (In later episodes, sponsors including Tower Records would be featured, introduced by George Liquor personally.) The crisp solid colors and shapes reflect the platform's vector art creation tools, but the expressions and characters are not far removed from their counterparts in *The Ren & Stimpy Show*.

Ren & Stimpy had already demonstrated the challenges of production in the traditional network model—its edgy content and hip audience appeal went downhill shortly after Kricfalusi was fired in 1992 and Nickelodeon took over production of the cartoon, and Kricfalusi posited that there was still a market for cartoons done his way. Kricfalusi wouldn't get another shot at the main *Ren & Stimpy* characters until 2003, when it was relaunched as *Ren & Stimpy Adult Party Cartoon* and for a three-episode run brought the sensibilities of Kricfalusi's Flash cartoons back to television. Flash offered a freedom from the production company model for creators like Kricfalusi, whose work didn't fit into the auspices of networks. The title alone, *The Goddamn George Liquor Program*, made its distance from corporate production cartoons immediately clear. "What you see every day on the street and laugh at, you aren't allowed to see in a cartoon. Well, now you can," Kricfalusi explained in an interview in *Wired* about the cartoon (Sullivan 1997). An installment of *George Liquor* required neither a professional animation team nor a studio's blessing for completion.

As the first in its genre, *The Goddamn George Liquor Program* was quickly noted for its significance. The series won the 1999 Annie Award for Outstanding Achievement in an Animated Interactive Production, with the following praise: "Freed from network interference, concerns about censorship and restrictive government regulation on how advertising can be incorporated into animated programming, John K has been able to experiment with new ideas to bring his unfiltered vision for the future of adult animation to his fans" (Animation World Network 1999). Judges even commended the series for introducing interactivity, as one episode included the game "Stuff the Duck in Jimmy's Butt."

The style of animation in *George Liquor* reflected the drawing tools of early Flash and some of what Manovich later called the style of "Generation Flash," with animated objects built on vector shapes and outlined images moving on distinctive tweens, resulting in a less distinctive shaping of characters than in *Ren & Stimpy*. Although only eight one-minute episodes of the program were produced, the web cartoon launched a new style of animation, which has since earned an unofficial nickname:

"Flashimation" (Daubs n.d.). The characterization of Flashimation in part was a procedural critique of methods—since the platform was accessible to amateurs, part of the expectation of Flashimation was that of low expertise: "How many amateur Flash artists are both accomplished at draftsmanship and also able to programmatically bind live XML data to a tree component? Not many. And that means that individual amateur Flash works tend to privilege one art creation paradigm option over others, not because users rationally match their paradigmatic choices to the materiality of their art and their message, but rather because users choose the tools with which they are the most competent" (Bardzell 2005). Early Flash users were animators, not technicians, and at this stage the Flash Platform encouraged solo production. Drawing and animating tools were integrated from the beginning, allowing one creator to work through each stage within the same program. While the drawing toolset predated the animation components, the animation toolset flows from the creation of elements.

However, there was some legitimacy to claims of Flashimation favoring certain aesthetic styles, as this preference was more clearly embedded in the vector drawing toolset at the platform's origin. The impact of Lev Manovich's "Generation Flash" on the future of animation would be seen in a reliance by many animators on simple shapes, sometimes sloppy aesthetic choices, and minimalism for the sake of expediency rather than as conscious design. But that same expediency would allow animation to take a new role in digital culture as a disposable, quickly-produced medium for memes and other short-lived content. One early Flash success story, *Homestar Runner*, was first created in *Mario Paint* by two students who started by making parody animations. Looking at the evolution of aesthetics in *Homestar Runner*, the characters kept their fundamental qualities. However, the smooth lines and simple textures reflect a style of Flash vector art that is both distinctive and easy to animate. The first Flash cartoon created by the *Homestar Runner* team used basic vector shapes that morph as the character bounces across the screen—a feat possible with only a few keyframes thanks to Flash's built-in tweening. By contrast, characters in the *Mario Paint* version of *Homestar Runner* move stiffly across the screen, their own shapes staying static and mostly changing only in positions relative to one another.

Homestar Runner, created by Mike Chapman and Craig Zobel while they were students at the University of Georgia, began as a children's storybook parody that eventually became a series of animations and games. The site is notable in that it was always hosted by the pair individually and was never supported by advertisers, instead relying on merchandising the "great athlete" Homestar Runner and his friends. While it is impossible to get a precise picture of amateur production over the last two decades, because much work is anonymous or pseudonymous and the sheer amount of amateur content is staggering, success stories such as this one exemplify the path of an amateur into the spotlight through web distribution and "viral" movement. Flash was pivotal to the development of the series, as it allowed Chapman and Zobel to participate in the same style of web series creation that Kricfalusi, a professional, had started. It suited the homemade look of the show. As Mike Chapman put it, "The introduction of Flash allowed non-animators like ourselves to fake our way through making cartoons" (Simpson 2006). Chapman and Zobel here draw a distinction between their work as amateurs and professional works, but credit the platform—used by professionals and amateurs alike—with their success. Ultimately, Flash's accessible animation tools allowed them to take their characters and progress from the simple bouncing movements of their 1999 "first flash" to character-driven animations with simple actions, voiceover, and recognizable characters such as Strong Bad, a wrestler prone to answering emails in one of the site's best-known animation series. Flash reached a broader audience thanks to characters like these, as the platform would become synonymous with these types of iconic works, easily and quickly shared through the emerging mechanisms of web 2.0, and consequently permeate pop culture memory.

In 2006, the creators of *Homestar Runner* celebrated Flash's tenth birthday with a cartoon extolling the virtues of Flash 5, the last version of Flash to keep the animation timeline at the forefront. The cartoon used the animation environment as a backdrop, praising the platform while mocking the inconvenience of some features: "Happy birthday, Flash 5!! And to a lesser extent 6, 7, and 8!! Oh, Flash 5, we've been through it all together, except when I needed to embed video" (Homestar Runner 2006). The thank-you card serves as a reminder of the influence the platform has had on its early adopters, who have often continued to produce animation primarily using Flash without deviation to another production environment. The focus on Flash 5 is also a reminder of the importance of the Flash player's backward compatibility, as the platform continued to allow creators to work and distribute in older versions of the development environment without limiting their audience. *Homestar Runner* itself saw many years of success, called "the most popular homegrown animation in the world" with "upwards of 200,000 visitors a day" at their peak, despite being what could be generously called "strictly do-it-yourself" animation (Wood 2003).

Beyond the Web

The cross-pollination of television and web-based cartoons would move back and forth across distribution and network boundaries. Flash appealed even to networks that hadn't traditionally invested in cartoons as a format, as the platform inherently didn't require the involvement of more than a few employees. The web's burgeoning hits also offered a clear wealth of potential goldmines, often created by students or would-be artists happy to see their shows moved onto networks or repurposed into the commercial space. *The Goddamn George Liquor Program* was almost licensed for Pontiac car commercials, and JibJab produced ads for Sony and Disney when not making Flash election parodies. JibJab's work is most recognizable for replacing Flash's vector art with imported imagery, often of politicians and their settings, while keeping the same style of transitional animation to use those characters as puppets on their animated stage. The authenticity associated with grassroots Flash animation—rising to popularity through crowdsourced approval, bringing a property to the attention of network executives rather than the other way around—briefly allowed Flash to occupy a novel space in animation. This occurred at the same time that scholars such as Henry Jenkins and Lawrence Lessig were noting the rise of participatory and remix culture, both of which were strongly present in the cut-and-paste style of JibJab and many other online Flash animators.

Both film and television were touched by Flash production, although the Flash platform's affordances did not always make it entirely well suited to these uses. *Lil' Pimp*, with such unlikely voice actors as William Shatner, would have been the first big budget Flash film spawned by a webcomic. Instead, it went directly to DVD. As one reviewer observed:

> As the first feature length movie made entirely using flash animation, Lil' Pimp at the very least has a unique selling point. Still, test audiences booked for the exits, pushing the theatrical release back two years before it finally arrived in the straight to DVD dump. While not as brazenly awful as you might expect (how bad can any movie featuring both the voice of William Shatner and Ludacris really be?), Lil' Pimp is basically one of those annoying, forcibly irreverent internet flash movies that some dude you hate emails you, only extended by 80 minutes. (Carter 2004)

Much of what the reviewer describes as characteristic of *Lil' Pimp* could be said of countless hours of animation on Newgrounds and other

Figure 2.1
Lil' Pimp, feature-length Flash production, 2005, Mark Brooks

Flash communities: however, animation produced within those communities not only does not attempt to reach a broader demographic, but also benefits from the assumptions of style that viewers bring to those portals. One problem faced by efforts like *Lil' Pimp* to bridge the gap between computer and theater was the incongruity of background and characters, as seen in figure 2.1. Flash's limited vector drawing toolset encouraged animators to create characters within the program while importing backgrounds and thus a difference in line weight and flow, as is clear in this screenshot, was one distinctive feature of Flashimation style. Improved importing capabilities through integration with Illustrator, including the preservation of layers, would still not fundamentally improve the workflow in separating foreground from background, resulting in occasionally jarring results in amateur productions. And while their algorithmic nature allows vector graphics to theoretically scale to any size, the amount of flat color and harsh outlined shapes is more jarring on a big screen, making Flash more suited to ports to television than the movie theater. The styles of computer animation successful in theaters (as perhaps best exemplified by the legacy of Pixar) would be both data- and process-intensive, delivering enough detail to construct recognizable identities and in some cases surprising realism. Also, most such computer animation is 3D—a step Flash would not take for some time, and never integrated particularly successfully, which we will touch on in chapter 5.

But the problem of expectations associated with Flashimation off-line wasn't merely aesthetic: the same assumptions of content followed from digital distribution networks to television. And often, with just cause, the same sensibility found on Newgrounds would make Flash the choice of many adult-oriented cartoons whose heirs are now dominating Adult Swim on the Cartoon Network. Most television Flash productions were directly spawned by web serials: in 2000, *Breakup Girl*, a superhero who fights against "crimes of the heart" with stories featuring "nice guys" and "desperately single" girls in online advice columns and comics, became the first Flash animation on TV when it was acquired by Oxygen and briefly aired despite some disputes over the appropriateness of the pilot episode for the network. This was only the beginning of Flash on television, as shown in figure 2.2. The Cartoon Network, a twenty-four-hour option for cartoons that started in 1996, would add Adult Swim in 2001. The first show featured in this new segment, *Home Movies*, was produced with Macromedia Flash following a first season produced in "Squigglevision," a

Figure 2.2
Breakup Girl, 1999, Lynn Harris and Chris Kalb

pseudo-animation style using oscillating lines in the place of tweening, to mixed reviews.

Networks appreciated the power of Flash when it came to avoiding the traditional demands of animation. Production studios filled with tweeners playing the role that the technology could cheaply fill. Individuals and small teams producing web shorts were similarly empowered. However, former Disney employee Phil Nibbelink demonstrated Flash's potential for longer-form productions in his feature-length film *Romeo & Juliet: Sealed with a Kiss* (2006). The film, at a length of 71 minutes, was animated entirely in Flash—and produced without any assistance. Nibbelink's accomplishment is most notable for its scale. As a professional animator, Nibbelink was already familiar with the processes and needs of hand-drawn animation, which he translated into the world of vector graphics with his two simply shaped seal lovers at the center. Nibbelink described his process and reliance on Flash's vector-based animation system for keeping the production manageable:

> I used Flash, because it draws with vectors. What I mean by that is, the computer understands a line in terms of its start point and end point and one point in the middle that creates the curve. What that allows the computer to do is output the line work to incredibly high resolution . . . I would put out these giant files that would go to the film recorder and those would be shot one frame at a time on film. But, for me, animating vectors keeps the files very small so I can go very fast. (Armstrong 2007)

The choice of seals for central characters allowed Nibbelink to use vector characters of relative simplicity, and it recalls the example Gay mentioned as one of the very first applications of Flash by his team: leaving most of the film's detail in the backgrounds. The 112,000 frames took Nibbelink, working alone, four and a half years to achieve—a staggering rate of production given the length of the film. His process highlights one of the essential differences between building in Flash and hand-drawing, as the scaling of images is eased by mathematical representations at work underneath the visual space. While much of Flash still lives online, this scalability to the style allows for continual porting and viewing quality even given the increasing size and resolution of monitors.

Timelines and Tweens

Even the earliest version of Flash put the metaphor of the timeline front and center in the user interface. The implementation of timeline animation in Flash was the natural extension of an already accepted practice in the animation industry: some frames matter more than others. The division between "keyframes" and "tweens" was traditionally one of labor, where the skilled animator would rely on less skilled artists to fill in the rest of the movement. Flash replaced those tweeners with automation, but the automatic generation does not have the same understanding of a particular object's motion, instead replacing it with a mathematical function that simplifies things like friction, weight, mass, and gravity. For innovators like the creator of Flash's first pinball game, that simple formula provided a foundation for experimentation, allowing "tweens" to replace the physics calculations of a pinball's progress while being guided by rules in frame jumping that resembled physical system constraints.

The Flash Player is a constantly evolving piece of software, adapting and expanding with new features and capabilities that are then provided as the authoring tools such as icons and eventually a scripting language. Despite the changes to the bytecode that runs within it and the virtual machine that interprets it, the SWF file format has remained largely unchanged, which is essential to the backward compatibility of the player. The virtual machine (or VM) interprets the bytecode in the same way an actual machine would interpret machine code designed for it. VMs are widely used in cloud hosting and are also a foundation of Sun's Java platform. SWF (pronounced "swiff") files, identified both by the extension ". swf" and the MIME type application/x-shockwave-flash, are optimized for scalability, simplicity, speed, and scriptability. They are constructed such that important information, like file size, number of frames, and frame size, comes first in a large file, and that the movie can begin being executed even before it has finished downloading. The layout of the file is divided into blocks of certain types, including the header, the FileAttributes tag, a number of tags, and the end tag. Tags can be either definition tags, such as shapes, text sounds, and bitmaps, or control tags. Each tag is executed sequentially, with definition tags assigning a unique ID (called a "character ID" and referred to as a character) to its content in a data structure called a dictionary. Dictionaries allow users to look up the location of some data chunk by key, and in this case store the keys in an order that makes it easy to insert or find an object by its key. Control tags (such as (ShowFrame, TellTarget, and PlaceObject) manipulate characters in prescribed ways. The Flash Player proceeds until it encounters a ShowFrame tag, where it then executes all of the actions accumulated and renders the current elements to the screen. The format is efficient because it stores the changes, or deltas, between the previous value for a property and its new value—and that efficiency translates into less-intensive processing and web-friendly files. These values include everything from position or height to alpha channel (for transparency) and color. If there is no change, the player will simply render the item if it is in the display list as it was in the previous frame. The creation and manipulation of frames within the timeline editor reflects this choice; when there are no frames between two keyframes, the objects do not change.

The definitions tag corresponds to those accessible within the authoring environment, including fills and strokes, symbols, and interface elements such as text areas and buttons along with the layer they are on. Symbols are important elements in the interface as well as in the data format; they refer to a character ID while retaining their own properties, allowing users to animate a symbol's position or scale independently. As Flash users attempted more complex development, this would be particularly crucial due to its performance characteristics, allowing games building on the concept of the pinball experiment to present multiple moving images and graphics on the stage as fitting into rule-based systems such as physics.

Frames are containers for the actions and objects displayed on them, and special keyframes and tweens are used to render the intermediate frames. Because each frame, and not just keyframe, has all of the properties for each element, the ability to see the results of the "in between" frames while stepping through the animation frame by frame is particularly important: this allows visual tweaking by an animator manipulating the timeline and refining the graphical representation. There were initially two types of tweens in Flash's authoring environment: motion tweens, which operate on symbols, and shape tweens. Motion tweens change the position of a symbol over time, and shape tweens require a vector shape to distort using a transformation. Between these two tools, one of the more time-consuming jobs of animation can be at least partially automated, allowing the machine to do the work that in hand-drawn animation would require intermediate tracers and the approximation of teams of laborers working frame by frame. Tweens can be further refined through the use of easing, which uses equations to specify how fast or slow a motion begins or ends.

Interpolation creates intermediate values between two other values and is the foundation of tweening. If a shape were created at location $x = 10$, $y = 20$ and then a new keyframe created on frame 5 at $x = 50$, $y = 100$, the position at each frame would be equal to the difference between the values divided by the number of steps. For these values, the intermediate positions shown in table 2.1 would be generated.

Table 2.1

Sample tweening values for position across frames

Frame	xPos	yPos
1	10	20
2	20	40
3:	30	60
4:	40	80
5:	50	100

Because of how object data is stored in SWF tags, the final size of an animation is the same whether it was hand-authored or created with the assistance of a tween. Adding the fact that most artwork in Flash is vector based makes the format a very compact representation for animations. The linear interpolation in table 2.1 is typical of many amateur Flash movies where the artists either hadn't learned the principles of "squash and stretch" or were concerned with the content more than the lifelike quality of the movements. Motion in the real world has subtle and distinctive variations; an object can accelerate or hesitate as a result of the interaction of forces. Flashimation often has a unique unreal quality to motion, as such transformations are the easiest to create within the platform.

The use of an easing function emulates the tradition in animation of describing how the motion is to be carried out. An easing function takes a beginning and ending value, along with a time step, and returns the given position. Easing is handled by a single set of integers initially, using either a straight line or a motion guide to control the position of the object. Another more complicated and powerful type of tween supported by Flash is the shape tween. A shape tween takes a single shape (which must not be a symbol) and interpolates each control point. Shape tweens are often combined with motion tweens, such as the emblematic squash and stretch applied to a bouncing ball, where the ball's shape compresses and expands at the same time as its position changes.

The Flash authoring tool introduced and improved upon the number and power of the commands available for manipulating symbols inside a movie throughout the Flash releases while gradually increasing the required amount of hand scripting (see table 2.2). These commands vary from accepting text input to starting a movie by clicking a button.

In addition to shape and position data, frames can have actions associated with them. An "action" is a set of commands associated with characters that gets executed when the "playhead" arrives at the frame. Actions can also set up "listeners," or functions that await user interaction to execute.

Table 2.2

Releases and features (Bouhlel 2010)

Release	Year	Description
FutureSplash Animator	1996	Initial version of Flash with basic editing tools and a timeline
Macromedia Flash 1	1996	A Macromedia rebranded version of the FutureSplash Animator
Macromedia Flash 2	1997	Released with Flash Player 2, new features included the object library
Macromedia Flash 3	1998	Released with Flash Player 3, new features included the MovieClip element, JavaScript plug-in integration, transparency, and an external standalone player
Macromedia Flash 4	1999	Released with Flash Player 4, new features included internal variables, an input field, advanced ActionScript, and streaming MP3

An example of a "listener" includes a function that awaits the "on pressed" event, or when the program detects a mouse click. Another action would be "Go To and Play," which moves the current frame to an indicated frame and plays the animation from there. Variable names and commands are all in different cases, including spaces, and in fact are referred to differently depending on whether you want to "Get" or "Set" a property. Referring to items in the movie is accomplished via a reference syntax similar to a file system, with relative paths using ".." (two dots), which is also used in many file systems to represent the next level up, and likewise each successive layer being separated by a slash ("/"). To access an instance named "girl" on the main timeline prior to Flash 5, you would use "/girl." To access a MovieClip "arm" that is a part of the "girl" instance, you would use "/girl/arm." This path is particularly important because all actions must be directed to a specific instance using the "Tell" command (Croteau 1999). The slash notation was later removed in order to support strong typing, but the notion of a hierarchical structure for display objects remained.

All commands, including specifying tweens, could initially be indicated using the drag-and-drop, point-and-click interface. Each symbol (or character) can act on its own and communicate with each other. These language and interface choices were designed to ease non-programmers into a tool that essentially creates code for execution, instructing them in how to create nonlinear content. The interface and the scripts themselves would change significantly with the advent of ActionScript 1.0 in Flash 5, where the timeline remained at the center of even scripted behaviors—the same version of Flash celebrated by the *Homestar Runner* team in its birthday card.

The early Flash platform certainly didn't lend itself to the needs of creators who wanted to create games akin to desktop experiences—nor was it the best choice of the aspiring, full-length feature film director, despite the few instances we've mentioned. The early Flash pinball experiment, while impressive, didn't allow for a more dynamic relationship with the user's choices and couldn't replicate many of the physical laws at work in a complex pinball game. Desktop games at the time had achieved greater complexity and immersive environments, and an interest in 3D graphics was already having an impact on the personal computer (PC) gaming market. Compared to the affordances of the PC in 1997—which saw the release of *Age of Empires*, *Ultima Online*, and *Quake II* for Windows systems—the use of Flash for game development or meaningful interactivity looked appallingly limited. Clearly, the platform's audience did not yet extend to professional game developers, as *Ultima Online* alone demonstrated a level of Internet-based massive multiplayer gameplay that the browser could not compete with. But for animators and amateurs, Flash's lack of complexity and small format offered a great boon, and the relatively lightweight nature of early Flash made it ideal for the correspondingly low speeds of network connections and limited bandwidth.

At this early stage in Flash's development, animation is both the most essential and supported feature of the platform. Each iteration of the tool and the runtime added complexity, with an expanding object model and scripting. The focus of Flash would likewise change, and amateur creators would see the platform move toward another type of user. Even animators would eventually be disillusioned by the platform:

> Well right now, it's made it easier for non-skilled artists to break into the business.
>
> So TV cartoons have become cheaper and more amateurish as a result.
>
> I think Flash is a temporary fix. It was a good thing for the internet because it allowed you to make animation with small file sizes, but it also makes "tweens" which really makes animation look cheesy. Too many people rely on it to make things mathematically smooth, which to me looks very fake and cold.
>
> It ought to be easy to make a program just for animators and build in classic principles, real brush and paint tools to make it easier for us to learn the things that the animators of the 30s took a decade to learn. (Simpson 2007)

But this condemnation of the usability implications of Flash was nothing compared to what was to come. Flash offered solutions to common problems that faced web developers still searching for the optimum balance between traditional media and the untamed wilderness that was the web. Flash could subsume traditional roles of HTML buttons and events, speeding ahead of the capabilities for sound and state management to inspire entire new classes of interactions on the web. Flash's initial pitch was to add interactivity and animation to web pages, coexisting with other elements such as JavaScript and form elements, but it was the scripting language ActionScript, and its ability to smooth over the increasingly turbulent differences between browsers, that would transform Flash from an animator's tool to a full-fledged meta-platform.

Distribution

Flash's format made it ideal for extending far beyond the Saturday morning cartoon tradition—and promoting an amateur hour. It encouraged fan production, or what Jenkins terms "participatory culture," often through the imitation of a style remembered from youth but viewed with an adult sensibility and lens (Jenkins 2006). Most important, it was a totally different economic scale. An individual could accomplish the work of a production studio. This freedom would have tremendous consequences for the aesthetics of the emerging form. Opening the process to anyone able to master the timeline was a demystification of the art of the moving image, akin to the deconstruction of a paper flip book. However, these completed works still needed to move from their amateur creator's personal computer to a wider audience, and this initially required the user to master the web technologies involved in digital distribution. Macromedia sought to further bridge the gap in procedural literacy required to produce web multimedia by building tools to intercede in the distribution coding.

Flash files allowed for nearly instant distribution with the addition of a web server. The relatively small file sizes of SWFs combined with easy integration into existing web files formed the basis for the format's popularity. Thanks to portals like Newgrounds, users could also post and thus distribute their content immediately to sites gaining in web traffic and popularity. Newgrounds, launched in 1995 by Tom Fulp, relies upon the stability of the SWF file format to automate content verification along with crowdsourced user approval to determine a content hierarchy. The documentary "Everything, by Everyone," currently in production by Nathan Kuruna, focuses on the role Newgrounds played in defining Flash animation as an artistic medium while providing a forum for user-generated content. Hubs like Newgrounds were particularly essential in the early portal-dominated content model of the World Wide Web, because many users came through frameworks such as AOL that heavily influenced site visibility and made it more challenging to find works scattered across the Internet. These distribution networks were a revelation to animation. Previously, the only networks for reaching an audience were tightly controlled by corporate media gatekeepers unlikely to ever offer the seal of approval to the type of projects early Flash animators flocked to create.

These early spaces of amateur exchange were essential to defining Flash animation. On networks designed for amateur creators, trends in content as well as style were critiqued as part of Flashimation's trend: "Specifically, Newgrounds animations popular media often feature complex yet silly juxtapositions of icons, from pop stars to video game heroes, in videos made with conspicuously low production values that rely heavily on primitives carefully managed in space and time. The well-drawn, emotionally serious animation at Newgrounds is the exception, not the rule" (Bardzell 2005). This type of critique echoes the suspicion that accompanies any technology that makes not only creation but also distribution accessible to more people. Creators such as the *Homestar Runner* team are participants in Lessig's notion of the hybrid economy, where distinctions are maintained between an economy of "sharing" and an economy of "commerce" (Lessig 2008, 177). The content of the Flash animations and games is shared, but the merchandise connects the project to commercial outcomes. Others never enter the commercial economy, and instead participate in remix culture, as named by Lessig: "Remixes happen within a community of remixers. In the digital age, that community can be spread around the world. They are showing one another how they can create . . . that showing is valuable, even when the stuff produced is not" (77). Much of Flash animation can be dismissed as repetitive and derivative, but the act of participating within the community gives these amateurs a voice regardless of their day job or lack thereof. In this space, the line between producer and consumer is blurred—a not-uncommon state on today's web, but one that Flash helped create.

Kricfalusi anticipated today's strongly participatory culture when he said in an interview in 1999: "I went to the Web because there's no network. If you have an idea, you don't have to ask for someone's permission to put it on. It's between you and the audience" (Sinclair 1999). Kricfalusi's experiments with this model haven't ended. In July 2012, he launched a Kickstarter to fund a ten-minute animated cartoon, "Can without Labels," featuring the return of George Liquor (Kricfalusi 2012). Notably, the funding campaign mentions the need to finish the animation including tweening, and thus is a return to hand-drawn animation but with digital tools used in production, funding, and distribution: an extension of the communal approach the Flash platform inspired taken outside the platform itself. The role of studio executives and television networks in the creative process is completely eliminated, just as Kricfalusi's first forays into Flash animation embraced. The accessible metaphor of the timeline, with its reliance on keyframes and processing rather than labor and data-intensive methods of traditional animation, transformed the expectations associated with both production and distribution of animation. These metaphors would remain the foundation of Flash even as it aspired to be a more general-purpose interactive tool, and thus Flash's legacy cannot be divorced from animation, or even from its early roots as a graphics program. While not the only method for producing animation, Flash's vector-based model and approach to resource management set the standard for quick-loading web animations that could be easily integrated into a complete website design—for better or for worse, to recall Jakob Nielsen's warning that Flash is "99% bad."

Introduction

Cheerful 8-bit music pipes out of the computer speakers as a red-capped plumber sporting overalls hops from bricks to clouds as the screen scrolls with his motion to reveal more of the cartoon landscape. Using the arrow keys, the player guides the plumber Mario away from chasms and man-eating plants to safer ground in his endless quest to rescue a missing princess. This type of gameplay is characteristic of a platformer, a genre where the player guides a character through reflex-driven landscapes filled with obstacles. *Mario* has made appearances on every Nintendo console from the Nintendo Entertainment System to the hand-held Game Boy series to the Wii. But this player isn't at a Nintendo console. Instead, she's loaded one of the many *Mario* imitations available on Flash, transforming browser and keyboard into a platform for the side-scrolling game. The detail of the reconstruction might convince a player that he or she is on the original console. The creator may have "ripped," or pirated, the sprites directly or painstakingly recreated some of the characters and settings. Levels call for the same strategies, and the arrow keys make an adequate substitute for the keypad of a Nintendo controller. But the underlying code and framework is entirely new, built to exploit the potential of Flash as a platform not just for animation but for interactivity and gameplay, with an ease of entry and publishing that allows an individual to reach an audience comparable to Nintendo's own. The Flash platform provided a legion of examples besides *Mario*, and many programmers learned the basics of programming by creating games very much like its platformer model.

As of July 2013, there are nearly five hundred games tagged "Mario" on Newgrounds: the *Mario* collection notes that "the character who has become more recognized than Mickey Mouse is also featured in more submissions than anyone else on Newgrounds!" (Newgrounds n.d.). These games range from direct ports of classic Nintendo games to original sagas with new characters and crossovers. The process of re-creating classic games in Flash makes them "spreadable" by taking advantage of the affordances of Flash: as defined by Joshua Green and Henry Jenkins, spreadability "represents an alternative to now widely deployed metaphors which describe how audiences engage with content . . . [stressing] the technical affordances that make it easier to circulate some kinds of media content than others, the social networks that link people together through the exchange of meaningful bytes, and the diverse motives that drive people to share media" (Green and Jenkins 2011, 109). Lawrence Lessig notes that studies show creators in "remix culture" are often gamers, used to relating to media as participants, not recipients (Lessig 2008, 80). Games inherently invite coproductivity, which Hanna Wirman defines as expressed primarily through both gameplay and acts external to gameplay (Wirman 2009). Flash is already positioned as a force in this participatory culture, but the introduction of readily accessible tools for creating and experiencing games would make it a center for the remix—despite the fact that Flash itself is not an open source platform.

The availability of these emulated and remade experiences allows for the replay of games whose original platforms have fallen into technical obscurity. The play and preservation of such games has been labeled as "retrogaming." Retrogaming is, as Jaakko Suominen notes, more than a desire to return to something: it is a "resource" fueling the production of interactive culture (Suominen 2008). Likewise Mario's adventures in Flash are more than just a nostalgic turn for the platform: they are an entry point into production and a testament of Flash's ability to empower individual authors to recreate games that once took larger production teams. Many Flash portals are dedicated to emulations or imitations of games ranging from classic arcade games to much-loved console games. This evokes Darcy DiNucci's notion of "web 2.0" as a "transport mechanism" made real in the ability to imitate, translate, and consequently transport players to different devices using Flash as a mediator. The role of unpaid, typically amateur, creators in spreading these experiences returns to Lessig's concept of the hybrid economy, as we previously discussed as thriving on Newgrounds through the sharing of animation in exchange for community status. In this case the "sharing" is clearly centered on others' intellectual property, particularly in works with high fidelity in their representation of the original game experience. Copyright holders are unwittingly the source material for a sharing community. For these, no legal protection is possible, as works are tenuously released under the premise that the original games are no longer sold commercially. Often this falls in the same space as emulators for classic systems, such as the Flash-based S/NESBox, which provides an interpreter for playing Nintendo Entertainment System and Super Nintendo Entertainment System ROMs through the browser.

Flash is far from the only platform used for emulations and imitations, but classic games are particularly visible in the Flash sphere and Flash works well as a chameleon imitating the original formats. Classic game remakes are part of the "spreadability" of the process of production. These games provide a common framework for tutorials and the act of learning to program, while providing the foundations for creative work as it moves beyond the remake. However, in this case the "remix" is valuable not only for how it shows what an individual can create but also for what it demonstrates is possible for others. The accessibility of the games as a frame of reference allows for an ease of communicating abstract ideas, such as collision detection, to an audience of new programmers. This is particularly important because the Flash platform grew from an animation tool to one with clear affordances for game development, and a scripting language existing and evolving in tension with the original visual interface of the timeline. Flash amateurs are encouraged to first dive into the platform through what resembles the process of "radical reconstruction," or rebuilding a game as a way to understand how it works—along with programming logic itself (Tearse et al. 2012). We'll look at the classic platformer mechanics and conventions as they are reconstructed and reinvented in Flash. The first game, and even more important, the first platformer that a programmer creates is a testament to their experience and a milestone for their own development. These same mechanics form the fundamental interactivity for many of the games that made Flash game sites as influential to the future of gaming as any home console.

While many early arcade classics have found a home within the Flash platform, Mario has inspired a particular fervor. This is in part due to the ease with which its basic mechanics map onto the tools and capabilities of the Flash authoring model: animations become MovieClips, whose current animation can be controlled with scripting. Collision detection has been accomplished with a variety of methods, ranging from the built-in functionality of the Flash Player to using low-level code to achieve pixel-perfect accuracy and performance. Mapping controls for a twitch-based platformer is also fairly uniform across implementations, providing movement and action keys. And, finally, the actual gameworld itself, its many obstacles and backgrounds, can be managed either within the interface by dragging MovieClips around, or created from a configuration file or a level editor built into the game itself. Within each of these core mechanics are the inspiration and satisfaction of creating a beloved game and of enabling interaction with objects represented in Flash's visual environment. Many Flash programming books rely on examples evocative of *Mario* or other classic games because of the satisfaction of recognizing the game in one's work. *Mario* games have not only achieved comparable playability to the original in Flash, but they have charted mash-ups and fan-made homages that push the boundaries of Flash's capabilities.

We'll examine the elements involved in re-creating *Mario* and other platformers in Flash as a gateway to understanding Flash's own evolution from a tool for animators to a tool for game makers and other interactive designers. While chapter two focused on Flash's initial affordance of the timeline, this chapter will consider Flash as it was built for programmers and particularly as a tool for learning programming. The accessibility of the platform as a "first" tool for learning programming is essential to its legacy, which must be understood not only as encompassing works built in Flash but also in the careers and development of programmers trained on Flash's development models. The tutorials and resources created for learning programming in Flash through game creation contain not only the framework for the fundamentals of game design and scripting but also the blueprint for many of the works created by first-time Flash developers.

Communities of Learning

Tutorials for making new versions of *Mario* (and other classic games) were often distributed through communities of learning that resembled the communities for sharing Flash works. Like the works of Flash production, these tutorials—whether web-based or video-based—were designed to be spreadable media. Many communities for sharing Flash production hosted their own forums for spreading knowledge, including Newgrounds. Many of the products of the community were ephemeral and have since vanished from the net, as Donna Leishman notes in her study of the Flash community and its early reliance on the unpaid efforts of dedicated "fan-boys" who pushed the platform forward and either shared (or reverse-engineered) code as part of that advancement (Leishman 2012). Several early hubs included Yahoo groups for Flash developers and the forums for organizations such as Friends of ED, an early publisher of many designer-oriented Flash books and showcases. Older sites such as Flash Kit hosted some of the first Flash tutorials, posted from 1999 to 2001 and focusing primarily on manipulating elements of the timeline and working with movie objects (Flash Kit 2001). Such forums were part of the open source and sharing spirit that is one of the strengths of the Flash community, even if the Flash platform itself has an uneasy relationship with open source that we will explore later.

In 2004, following the release of Flash MX2004, users noted the primary shift of the community focus from forums and newsgroups to blogs (Kristin 2004). Many early developer resources were hosted and provided by the company itself: prior to the Adobe acquisition in 2005, Macromedia maintained its own developer center that included a tutorial on making Asteroids using the Flash drawing API and ActionScript (Macromedia, Inc. 2002). Those resources and tutorials that were deliberately circulated or repackaged for publication survive and offer a digital legacy of solutions to common programming challenges in the early days of Flash scripting and beyond. Actionscript.org, a dedicated site for discussion of and articles on Flash, hosts nearly five hundred tutorials posted primarily between 2005 and 2012. Several sites are the work of dedicated individuals: Lee Brimelow's gotoAndLearn.com hosts approximately one hundred tutorials on Flash based on ActionScript 3.0 alone along with an expansive archive of Flash 2.0 tutorials, while Trevor "Senocular" McCauley runs his own extensive site including a range of source files and extensions. Many of these tutorials are in video form, which is particularly valuable for Flash works that require manipulating not only the script but the physical interface of Flash's visual timeline editor. Several sites rose to provide tutorials dedicated to the needs of Flash game designers, including FlashGameTuts.com, which used both ActionScript 2.0 and ActionScript 3.0 for tutorials aimed and using minimalist graphics to build common genre games such as tower defense. More recently in 2009, ASGamer.com launched with a focus on building mechanics influenced by popular games and genre trends, such as implementing explosions and making Asteroids-style motion.

These tutorials are very much in the tradition of cookbook style guides, in that they focus on either implementing a particular design element in Flash or building portions of a larger project. There is no standard format for a community tutorial, but the inclusion of the source code and un-compiled files is common practice to allow referencing of the final product. Often tutorials are based on reverse-engineering a desired mechanic or sharing a successful project element to allow others to move forward with the design. One tutorial series by Ben Reynolds on the As3 Game Tutorial website focuses on complete games broken down into steps, such as scrolling the background or animating the character. These tutorials are not meant to replace or even be the same quality as published books, and Reynolds makes that clear in his disclaimer:

> DISCLAIMER: I am not teaching the most efficient, technically-accurate, professional way to make a platformer. Rather, I am going to show you how to make a game that is easy to understand, achieves quick results, and will teach you many concepts which are vital to understand if you wish to create a more complicated game. (Reynolds 2011)

These sort of tutorials are only rarely limited in their accessibility: many Flash instruction books launched websites for openly sharing the code samples discussed in the books, and the limited-access Flash events were often recorded and shared online. Any new developer seeking to build an observable game mechanic could likely find a starting point in the explosion of community resources over the past decade.

While a full discussion describing the various methods for teaching programming is beyond the scope of this book, the typical tutorials that teach programmers how to create *Mario*-like games reveal a great deal about both how the underlying Flash Player works and how it was understood by developers new to the platform. Other platforms have taken a similar approach to the early Flash interface's use of blocks describing programming elements. As Flash evolved, Adobe decided to move away from its first tight integration of the timeline, objects and code, in favor of two separate development ideologies, designer-focused and developer-focused through the two products, Flash Builder (formerly Flex Builder [2006 onward, the product name was changed in 2009 to Flash Builder]) and Flash Professional ("Professional" added to its name in 2007 with Adobe's acquisition, and further was rebranded to fit with the rest of the Adobe product line).

The following sections take a look at each of the required elements for creating platformers traditionally taught by tutorials and enabled by the Flash runtime. The features described are used to create a game that can be identified as a *Mario* game, both in their implementation in Flash and their implications for how Flash enabled the creator's growth in the conventions of procedural media and games. As Flash moved from its first steps in "actionscripting" to the more recent (as of 2013) embrace of three-dimensional (3D) accelerated graphics, the persistence of these core proficiencies in mastering the Flash platform remain consistent. Though the platform increasingly favored implementations using libraries and counseled programmers to avoid mixing timeline code with classes, the majority of amateur creation still relies on these methods to create satisfying experiments and homages for publication on sites such as Newgrounds.

The choice of language for these tutorials is incredibly significant as it reveals the disjoint interests of the community of creators and the stewards of the platform. A large number of tutorials focus on ActionScript 2.0, even though Adobe officially stopped supporting the language. User "deathink" on Newgrounds posted this in response:

> People have only scratched the surface with as2. I hear a lot of people talking bad about it, say it's old and out dated. But it's my programming medium, I enjoy programming in as2. It's like someone coming up to me and saying "Matthew, why do you spend so much time painting in oil paints, when you can just use a camera. Don't you know cameras are newer and faster?"

We'll revisit this comparison of ActionScript 2 to an artistic medium in chapter 5, with the discussion of Flash and new media art. However, the continued interest in ActionScript 2.0 can also be connected to its relative accessibility, both in comparison to ActionScript 3.0 and to other scripting languages. Flash scripting support has evolved haphazardly, adopting at times some of the best features from dedicated programming environments. These features allow programmers to be more efficient: they enable them to stop the code at any point in its execution and to see the inner workings of variable values and output during execution. The scripting environment in Flash CS3 requires a number of leaps for a novice programmer, especially connecting the objects onstage with the concept of an instance and with the even more confusing (yet still compellingly powerful) idea of a Symbol. The decision to price newer versions of the software and language out of the reach of amateur creators left many seeking alternatives. Flash CS3 and MX are maintained and developed on despite more recent releases of Flash Professional.

Guiding a programmer through tasks is especially important even with the presence of video tutorials, and Flash provided continual support for programmers through a script reference and internal prompting. This was originally a default and part of the normal mode when working with Flash 4 onward, but it was separated and labeled as the "Script Assist" feature with the release of Flash Professional in 2007. This form-based programming tool works like a dictionary of templates that prompts for identifiers or data necessary to specify how the generic fits in and which variables should be referenced. The tool also describes any line of code and, when used exclusively, eliminates syntax errors such as improperly nested brackets and missing semicolons. The early integration of this support system implies the expectation of an amateur or unfamiliar developer as a primary user, while the later version of the Script Assist as an optional tool suggests Adobe's desire to meet the needs of a more dedicated developer base while maintaining access to newcomers.

Script Assist requires knowledge on the part of the user to fill in "not_yet_set" holders that appear from the template. The concept of an assistant to coding evolved into Code Snippets, which populates the templates with references to currently selected objects on the stage. These snippets range from loading text from an external file to handling events such as mouse or keyboard presses. Starting in Adobe's Flash CS3, the ability to use auto-completion was added, bringing one of the more powerful features that programmers rely on to a tool aimed at designers. Unlike Script Assist, autocompletion uses the compiler's knowledge of the current scope and the valid parameters to prompt the programmer with a possible completion of the current identifier being typed. Because of the complexity of scope in the Flash Professional environment, this can be tricky and there are numerous reports of reliability issues, especially when considering namespaces from custom libraries. Even so, Script Assist represents an effort to reach the amateur programmer through tools that ease the acclimation to the library and often confusing syntax required by Flash and AS3.

These characteristics, internal reinforcement and tutoring, are common to development environments intended for classroom or introductory use. When combined with the human readability of ActionScript as a high-level language, these tools were also very designer-friendly and reinforced some of the visual elements of building in Flash. As both a widely distributed and widely taught language, Flash blazed a path in both providing a reason to learn coding as well as a variety of entry points into programming.

Platformer Tutorial

New developers and designers learning Flash inevitably came across gaming tutorials, particularly as commercial applications of Flash grew to include advertisement and sponsor-based exposure through quick web games such as platformers. They might have even stumbled on a tutorial for how to create a game when searching for the game itself. YouTube lists that there are about 143,000 results for a search for "Flash Platformer Tutorial," suggesting that this recognizable genre offers a strong common grounds for would-be designers looking to learn how to develop for Flash. The majority of the tutorials are written for AS2, despite the 2006 introduction of AS3 with the release of Flash Player 9. ActionScript 2.0 remains the most popular language for beginners learning Flash, owing to its forgiving syntax and the intuitive way of associating scripts with objects. Platformer tutorials provide a useful lens onto the particular ways that Flash contributed to procedural literacy, and the affordances of the platform itself lent itself to "spreadability."

Programmers can approach developing Flash works in one of two ways: a timeline-focused approach, where they use MovieClips to represent game objects, or a code-focused approach, which uses classes, data structures, and symbols and avoids the interface. The code-focused approach often is more intimidating, because the tutorials consist of a great deal of code snippets and programming theory. The timeline approach is ideally suited to video tutorials, as most of the interactions are visual.

A simple platformer tutorial consists of how to create a character MovieClip, controlled by the keyboard, which navigates a screen populated with a second type of MovieClip, the eponymous platform. These two components correspond to figure and ground, or setting and actor. Central characters in platformers' act as the player's avatar: as Bob Rehak discusses in his study of game avatars, such characters "merge spectatorship and participation" and are central to creating games in this genre (Rehak 2003). Likewise, Flash video tutorials allow new developers to be spectators viewing others' creativity within the development environment while following along and building their own variation on the given formula.

Many tutorials are identical to one another and are written/recorded more as an exercise. Flash tutorials share some structure with other programming tutorials, though the visual output and the direct manipulation of assets lends itself to videos. The author typically starts with a demonstration of the finished product and then breaks down the programming tasks into discrete phases, such as drawing a character, manipulating the interface and copying and pasting code and testing the movie. The tutorial actions don't always follow the missteps and mistakes that occur with actual development but instead provide a streamlined presentation of the act of creation. Any libraries or code samples are provided, though sometimes transcribing the code is a recommended part of the learning process.

However, the outcome resembles "How to Draw" style books, guiding the learner into a series of increasingly satisfying approximations of a beloved game.

An exception to the typically screencast or screenshot led tutorial is the *in situ* tutorial. One such tutorial created was a collaboration between Newgrounds community members "Actionsick," "ZRB," "DawnOfDusk," "NYSKA," "KevnSevn," and "Knysezekanimated" (ActionSick et al. 2008). Their tutorial uses elements in the movie to reveal the properties and characteristics of the elements displayed. After completing this plat-former tutorial, the player will have copied the steps necessary for moving an avatar around an environment, avoiding obstacles and (in more advanced versions) orchestrating automated camera movement to follow the player.

The ways in which newcomers to the platform are taught how to use it reflects on the core metaphors and the ease with which they are under-stood. Flash established itself as a medium not only because of the ease with which its content can render, but also by the ways its user communi-ties were able to grow and welcome newcomers. The platformer provides the ritual for this indoctrination—an object of joy and an achievement to complete. All begin with the character avatar and the objects that define the ground and how they become related with the player's input.

Input and Movement

Navigating a space with an avatar defines a platformer even more than the jumping and collision detection. The arrow keys provide a convenient analog to the D-pad of more traditional console controllers, though first person shooters have popularized the more compact left-hand version (WASD). Many provide a set of action buttons used to jump or activate a secondary ability, typically the shift or ctrl keys. Tutorials, like new games in the genre, are generally very faithful to this control scheme expectation. Studies of player control systems reveal that these simple controls can be essential to creating a feeling of immersion thanks to their familiarity and thus are often consistent across titles and platforms (Cummings 2007). Likewise, Flash relies on consistent conventions for manipulating visual objects and movie clips in its interface as part of building experiences—for instance, clicking to select an object, having a secondary panel appear that describes additional properties. The implementation of a game, like the first few images encountered in the very first levels of a platformer, is revealed incrementally.

The first authoring task is to accommodate the player's input, which imbues the player's will into the character and solidifies their identification. This authoring task requires relatively little understanding in Flash of the calculations of pixels, bounding boxes and rendering taking place in the Flash Player behind the scenes. The steps to implement a game are consistent across Flash tutorials: the code checks, at each frame, whether one of the three arrow keys are held down (or a jump button). This is done either continuously (as in AS2 to check the state of the button) or by checking a variable that has been set by a keyboard event handler. One way to move the character is to change the avatar's position based on whether the left or right arrow keys are currently pressed. The result of changing the MovieClip's position via code is as immediate and tractable as clicking and dragging a symbol around in the Flash Professional interface, except in this case the user is granted the control. The player pressing the key that is designated for "jump" can also be detected, moving the character up by decreasing the property "y" of the MovieClip continuously. While some tutorials take the player into other possibilities, these are the foundation on which the simulation is architected: players provide input, the game processes the inputs and code changes element properties. The real work is still done by the platform, handling the display of the bitmap, maintaining a reasonable frame rate and processing and dispatching the operating system's notifications of keyboard input.

From the novice developer's perspective, there are two options for how to code the necessary procedures. With ActionScript 2.0, code is attached to a variety of structures, either on a frame in a movie clip or on the movie clip itself. In his guide to ActionScript, Colin Moock breaks apart the usages of movie clips into several unofficial categories that fulfill functions later addressed by more standardized methods, classes and event handlers in ActionScript 3.0 (Moock 2001). For example, code which is executed every frame is often called the "main loop" in game programming. To achieve this in ActionScript 2.0, a programmer would create a MovieClip object whose purpose was to organize this repeated code execution and inside it attach a procedure, which handles the "enterFrame" event. Handling an event means listening to messages sent specifically to an object for a type of event, often represented as a string such as "enterFrame" or a static variable name that contains the string, such as "ENTER_FRAME."

In the mind of the programmer, such distinctions dissolve into a concept of continuous execution, especially when dealing with simple statements or tests. The following code describes the test for whether a key is pressed, and is executed once per frame when attached to a movie clip. When placed on a frame, the code is executed every time that frame is played.

The method for handling a mouse event on a MovieClip in Action-Script 1.0 is similarly legible:

```
If(Key.isDown(KEY.<KEY>) {
//<Code to execute>
}
onClipEvent(mouseDown) {
trace("onPress called");
}
```

ActionScript 1.0 mouse event listener

In the case of the attached script (above), the condition on which action takes place is explicit and is legible even to a novice, reflecting the human readable intent of ActionScript itself. It says, "If a specific keyboard button is pressed, do something."

```
// This line registers the function to be called when the event
// is triggered on the current object.
addEventListener(KeyboardEvent.KEY_DOWN, keyHandler);
addEventListener(KeyboardEvent.KEY_UP, keyHandler);
// Changes state based on the type of code and type of event.
function keyHandler(event:KeyboardEvent):void {
if(event.keyCode==Keyboard.RIGHT && event.type ==
KeyboardEvent.KEY_DOWN)
{
// Record the fact that the right key is now down
} else if (event.keyCode==Keyboard.LEFT
&& event.type == KeyboardEvent.KEY_DOWN) {
// Record the fact that the left key is now down
}
}
```

ActionScript 3.0 Event Handler

When ActionScript 3.0 introduced a more standards-based implementation of event handlers, it also introduced a more verbose structure to accomplish the same result. A programmer would need to first create a separate "handler" or "event listener" procedure, usually with logic to distinguish which type of event occurred, and then register it with the Flash Player to run when it detects a keyboard event from the operating system. This makes explicit what is taking place behind the scenes and provides a more uniform handling over special purpose function names such as onPress. The downside, as in much of programming, is an increase in the amount of boilerplate code and an increase in the amount of programmer knowledge required to begin.

Some of the most efficient uses of event listeners were not common. Optimizing calls by using a function tables, remembering to remove event listeners when finished with them and ensuring the correct traversals of the display list are all possible improvements enabled but not regularly used with the newer event system. This could be a reason why the simpler, though more error prone, methods of ActionScript 2.0 were preferred by some users even as late as 2013 when AS2 was removed from the options of Flash Professional. Once the programmer was able to move a MovieClip across the screen, the cycle of resolving the gap between what is currently happening and what "feels right" begins. Achieving a satisfying experience involves more than directly tying input to output, however.

Movement in a Flash game involves checking the state of the keyboard and calculating the world's objects and positions. The important objective was to make the player feel as if his or her avatar were inhabiting a two-dimensional (2D) world, one whose rules suggested forces present in our own experience, such as gravity, friction, and momentum, and rules that enforced boundaries and interactions such as a ground plane and walls. Flash, in a few "built-in" procedures and capabilities provides the necessary handles to create very simple approximations of platformers. When these limitations are embraced, understood and surpassed through custom, game-specific logic, they can compete in performance and popularity with many console games and have created one of the most important genres of the past decade: casual games, discussed in the next chapter. The underlying problems of platformers and physics games are the same: calculating position and relevant boundaries, updating only those elements that have changed and making the experience feel smooth and responsive.

Acceleration, Friction, and Gravity

In Flash, as discussed in the previous chapter on animation, "tweens" are an interface for animators to specify a smoothly interpolated transformation that takes place from a beginning and ending frame. In a game that must respond to player input, the exact position cannot be known ahead of time. The exact trajectory must be calculated and used to determine the position in each frame, as at any point a player could press or release a button or an enemy or environmental hazard could intervene. While the simple version of increasing speed and applying friction will enable movement, and can even be used in a piece of code executed on each frame to increment the position until a collision occurs, the smoothness of the movement will be disrupted by the discrete and uneven nature of how

Flash handles frame rate. At the level of a Flash movie, an author can request Flash to maintain a given frame rate, such as 30, but during execution many events either within Flash or the environment can change this. These factors can vary the actual time between frames as much as -10/+5 ms, limiting the fidelity of the gameplay to the programmer's intentions.

Many platformers accept this method as satisfactory, while others turn to the calculations a tween handles to determine the correct position of an object traveling, even when it isn't being rendered. These methods involve one of two solutions: calculate the elapsed time exactly, and adjust the simulation, or create a regular interval that is occasionally rendered. Flash provides access to the system clock both in the form of events that fire after a period of time as well as access to the current time. Using either of these, the correct positions for all moving objects in a simulated space can be calculated. At this point the notion of a frame becomes more fluid. Instead of a box on the timeline to be filled with designs and instructions, the simplicity of how the world works is brought into focus as not satisfactory, revealing another level of understanding required: physics and, significantly, the simulation of a world where physics has been contorted and manipulated.

Underlying the caricature of physics present in 2D platformers are nuggets of expressive procedures and spaces for code to determine how one game differs from another. Important questions that may not have been considered in the first games a player engaged with become relevant and demanding answers: how fast should the character move? How quickly should they fall, and what part of the character should indicate contact? These questions constitute the soul of an arcade or console game, and were the subject of both trial and error and taste. The feel of a platformer is directly attributed to the tuning these parameters and creating the timing and rhythm required to master obstacles using them. From the hellish levels of *Super Meat Boy* to the physics-defying puzzles of the 3D platformer *Portal*, the creative range of these basic mechanisms defines the entire genre. In the case of Portal, these mechanics have been back-ported into the two-dimensional world through Flash, even including the plausible extensions of physics brought to bear: transporting, while conserving momentum, through connected portals (We Create Stuff 2007).

Gravity is of great importance when working with a platformer such as Mario, and is generally easy to implement: determine, at each interval, whether the player avatar is in contact with a horizontal surface or airborne. If the player avatar is in the air, then have the player avatar accelerate downward until a fixed maximum. Otherwise, calculate movement, friction, and collision on the x-axis. One of the hallmarks of Mario's feel is the ability to determine jump height by the length of the press of the jump button. In some ways this anti-gravity and midair control of ascent is unrealistic, but its control makes for far more interesting gameplay obstacles (and interesting cheats, such as midair jumping enabled by Game-Genie). These fundamental simulations can be accomplished in any platform, and so this genre can be represented on any platform. The Flash Platform's core classes and libraries lend itself to a higher-level representation for beginners, while providing access to the underlying memory, pixels, and variables that older consoles relied on for their look and feel.

Collision Detection

Who knew that a flower could grow from a question mark? Through experimentation and through convention, the vocabulary of modern platformers was developed: interaction with objects occurred through collision. It was easier than parsing natural speech, and it lent to the tensions introduced by timers and physical menaces. It also constitutes one of the greatest challenges of implementing a system that includes gravity and solid bodies. One method for calculating collisions loops through all of the possible candidate objects that could possibly collide, determines whether they are in fact colliding, and responds appropriately. With the speed of modern processors, even a virtual machine can handle this feat easier than early hardware. The difficult has shifted from working within highly constrained memory and timing limitations to the difficulty of formulating instructions quickly and accurately. The implementation for collision detection varies greatly depending on whether the author uses the timeline or a more procedural approach, and especially if the Display List functionality provided by the Flash Player is embraced or discarded in favor of a more specialized alternative.

The Flash Player has offered a hitTest function for display objects since early versions. It is called on a MovieClip with a target DisplayObject or point with the result indicating if it overlaps or is contained in the MovieClip. It provides both a bounding box version and a shape-specific version. This method alone may seem all that is necessary to detect collisions, but the same interpolation that made movement lifelike also enables objects to bypass one another, go too far or miss an intended collision entirely. The exact position and the orientation of contact become important, as well. Mario is vulnerable from the sides and even from above, but his ability to stomp most enemies and pulverize bricks with his head defines the affordances and possible solutions to any player of the series.

There are several methods of calculating this interaction, and most of them owe much to the knowledge from the days of console games. One particular article dates from 1993, describing how a team implemented a platformer on the NES and references the key points of contact and how they solved the constraint problems associated with the platform. Modern Flash games aspire to this level of fluid gameplay, even though the vast majority rely on built-in functions such as hitTest. Often times the performance hit of using hitTest can interfere with the gameplay, and simplifications are necessary. All Display Objects in Flash can also be represented as a native Rectangle. When an object's position is represented by a Rectangle, regardless of the depth of the object, Flash will calculate whether two share common pixels when the intersect method is called.

By implementing these solutions, the programmer gains insight into the possible variations. Super Meat Boy was originally prototyped in Flash as Meat Boy (McEntee and McMillen 2008). The idea of sliding down walls came to be appreciated as an additional level of challenge based on gravity and the observation that many traditional platformer puzzles are based on timing challenges. Flash experiments have provided an opportunity to play with genre conventions, explore their limits and providing a low-risk way to explore their reception. Detecting intersection of elements on screen is an important capability in interactive simulated experiences, giving the abstract shapes properties and predictability that extends beyond their surface representation. The capability alone is not enough to reproduce the feel of more conventional platforms, but the progression enabled programmers to find increasingly accurate and expressive ways to represent collisions. Flash's role in enabling new genres of casual games was established through the ease with which the surface capabilities were understood and the solutions it revealed to the core problem of collision detection and handling brought the genre of platforms well into the next generation of games.

Tiling

Mechanical reproduction allows an artist greater leeway with creation; a single sound file may be played thousands of times, and the same image in a sprite-based game may accompany a player for dozens of hours of gameplay. Creating a simple *Mario*-style game does not require a tiling engine. In fact, the entirety of a level can be created using special purpose MovieClips and a single large background (also known as art based games). The need to reuse art in backgrounds and consistently map art to game elements in a game underlies the choice for a method such as tiling to create an expansive world in which to set a game, while conserving artist time and computer resources. Tiling is not the simplest way to create a platformer, but it quickly becomes a necessity for longer games especially as a way to optimize the use of resources.

Working under extreme resource constraints can be a source of inspiration. Mario's own evolution was strongly shaped by the technology available for each of his iterations, as Steven Jones and George Thiruvathukal describe in their platform study of the Nintendo Wii: "everything about the design of the original *Mario*, from using the arcade cabinet's button to make the plumber jump to the titular character's basic appearance, was shaped by the circumstances of the hardware and software available at the time of each of his incarnations. The platform helped to determine the artistic design" (Jones and Thiruvathukal 2012). This interdependence of genre evolution and the constraints of the platform can be seen in the earliest examples of digital games hardware. In *Racing the Beam*, Montfort and Bogost describe how constraints inherent in the Atari 2600, including the timing of the scan lines and the limited amount of memory allowed for sprites and game state inspired creative procedural aesthetics (Montfort and Bogost 2009). Part of the motivation behind innovating on a limited system was the large audience of owners. The same motivation underlies amateur and even professional Flash development, but unlike fixed hardware platforms, the Flash Platform evolved both in capability and performance along with its developers. While more recent computers have greater memory to handle larger assets or more CPU power, the fact that users must download all of the assets before playing a game and handle other tasks at the same time make these constraints again important factors in designing experiences close to those created by dedicated hardware and physical cartridges and media.

The content in a tiling system is stored as references to procedures and bitmaps that can be defined once and, through an efficient loop and data structure, be used a hundred times. One tutorial describes the two-dimensional array as the defining data structure. Arrays store a number of values in a sequence that can be accessed by an integer. These values can be numbers, representing a type of tile associated with a collision flag and an image. By keeping all of the assets in a grid, the way in which the game is stored mirrors the structure of the game universe itself. The necessary procedures can then be decided based on which tile is involved: rules such as gravity and the interaction of objects in the world can change whether it's a sky tile or a water tile. A ground tile can be a ground tile not only to Mario or the hero, but also to the enemies he encounters.

One of the first optimizations that Flash's file formats provided was to reference a single bitmap in multiple places. This lends itself perfectly to games where common elements reoccur frequently throughout the game. Flash introduces, like the timeline, specialized terms such as the symbol (a concept close to a class, but often taught as a template for a MovieClip to be created from). However, in order to fully capitalize on a tiling engine's configurability, the stage and its ease of authoring via the Flash stage and timeline interface must be abandoned. Instead, the data must be stored and reconstructed from an array or file. Inside that array are references to a table of tiles, some of which may be "sky" tiles; some may even be blocks that can be moved or destroyed. Each reference is used to retrieve the appropriate procedures and image for that location in the game. One method of handling tiles is to maintain a single tile with multiple frames. These frames can contain the possible background, and each reference is a label representing the art to show when the tile is present. An advantage to this approach is the ability to animate tiles, possibly storing a set of frames and looping them for a given tile.

The ease of authoring a Flash game was clearly not enough for some game authors. Instead, Flash has been used to create authoring environments for games that are firmly in an established genre. These authoring tools range from simple tile editors to more complicated authoring environments similar to that of GameMaker. One example of a successful Flash game creation tool is Sploder (Gaudrealt 2004). Sploder appeals for educational uses because of the possibility of incorporating physics and the necessity of testing and understanding. However, it does not make code the primary output, but rather the ability to save the results of the authoring tool and invite others to play the creation, not unlike Newgrounds. Sploder's mission statement embraces amateur creativity and a philosophy of spreadable media: "We believe that the world can be changed by creative people who use their minds to make the world better. By offering a place where people are rewarded for creativity in the context of games and play, we hope to point them toward a path to a more creative future" (Sploder 2004). Like Flash, Sploder has gone through several iterations, with a complete expansion in 2008 that added a forum for those using the platform to connect and share ideas.

Flash's role as a game authoring tool has even been addressed by academics interested in the ability of games to communicate complex topics. Game-O-Matic (Bogost et al. 2010) is a tool that enables authors without programming experience to create short, simple games based on concepts, such as those found in comics based on current events. These games take advantage of simple relations between words to instrument a wider variety of game mechanics, but as a result offer less control over the experience itself. Unlike Sploder, Game-O-Matic attempts to reach an audience of non-gamers to create games about "current events, your personal interests, or pretty much anything." Flash was chosen to represent these experiments in procedural rhetoric, capable of being generated and playable as a familiar form immediately.

Flash's evolution away from user-friendly interfaces has also accompanied its evolution toward the creation of interfaces for non-coders. The barriers to understanding how the platform works have been abstracted into more and more standardized engines that have a logic entirely different from their underlying representations. These platforms sit on top of Flash, enabling specific types of experiences and, more important, include the tools to author outside a Flash development environment. The variety of levels at which Flash can be authored represents the cumulative knowledge of both its users and those coming from other platforms. This knowledge can be represented as ready-made tools, but the most flexible solutions are shared in the form of libraries.

Libraries

Many of the optimizations described in this chapter are out of the reach of even dedicated developers wanting to create a game in a reasonable time period. For these, libraries offer a convenient, tested solution to problems such as collision detection and performance in exchange for less control. Libraries are interrelated classes, sometimes precompiled, that provide a new set of APIs (application programming interfaces, or the functions that provide access) on top of the Flash Player. The developers of the library often create tutorials specifically to demonstrate the use of the library, and it is standard to include example applications. Libraries enable developers to focus on the content and the organization of their own code, and often replace or enhance the basic capabilities of the Flash Player, such as a library for programmatic tweens. While libraries aid with the bookkeeping of assets and mathematics calculations, the authoring experience remains the same. All libraries can be included in a number of Flash authoring environments after the introduction of ActionScript 3.0, including both Adobe Flash Builder (and its predecessor, Adobe Flex Builder) and the open source, Windows-based FlashDevelop. Adam Saltsman developed a new library for building Flash games for ActionScript 3 called Flixel, first released in 2009. Flixel's affordances include built-in tools for handling mouse and keyboard input, and one of the most comprehensive introductory tutorials is for creating an "EZPlatformer" (Saltsman 2011). We'll revisit these libraries and the impact they have on creative Flash works in later chapters.

Conclusion

Remaking *Mario* wasn't enough for some of the most dedicated Flash creators. The *Super Mario 63* fangame, released in 2009 and finalized in 2013, uses both familiar and original levels as part of a long battle of Mario against Bowser. The elaborate world begins with an animation sequence showing a layered platformer complete with animated enemies and visual stimuli in the foreground and clouds in the background. The most innovative feature is the inclusion of a level designer that offers players the ability to build and share their own Flash levels using familiar *Mario* sprites and tiles. The process of level creation as shown is once more removed from coding, keeping only the visual elements of a Flash-like interface and allowing player-designers to work within the constraints of the original mechanics. The game includes a dedicated level-sharing site with nearly two thousand additional levels as of July 2013. Some are remakes of worlds from existing games, while others build entirely new and unexpected locales. The system and its sharing are reminiscent of a more limited version of the editor included with *Little Big Planet*, a commercial title from Sony with similar roots.

The use of classic games as a shared foundation for the community also has its dark side. Alongside a next generation of seemingly classic side-scrollers featuring a remixed *Mario* are games such as *Mario KKK*, which Andrew Selepak notes as exemplary of the type of modified classic games produced by a community of developers who replace traditional enemies with members of minority groups (Selepak 2010). The accessibility and adaptability of the original mechanics make it possible to transform the platformer for a variety of purposes, some of which we will examine in chapter 5 as part of the art game movement. There is also an entire category of new games that borrow aesthetics from classics, which Kayali and Schuch refer to as the oxymoronical-sounding "contemporary retro game" (Kayali and Schuh 2011). Flash guides even devoted attention to how to create those games. Jeff Fulton and Steve Fulton included a section on the subject in their guide to making Flash Games with Action-Script 3.0, introducing the genre as "post-retro . . . games that utilize a retro aesthetic mixed with both retro and modern gameplay elements to create a wholly new experience" (Fulton and Fulton 2010, 474). Some of these influences would play a strong role in the development of casual gaming and amateur game development in Flash, moving from platformers to the fusion of gaming genres.

Among dozens of game creation toolkits and libraries, two development environments in particular stand out for how they facilitate the creation of Flash-like games: GameBuilder and Unity. GameBuilder offers a graphical user interface (or GUI) focused method of experimenting with game mechanics and creating two-dimensional (2D) games. Unity integrates all of the engine features at the same level as the interface itself. The Unity editor was created to ease the creation of 3D games, enabling players to jump into a game and tweak variables in a form-like interface while the game is running. Unity also enables export to more platforms than Flash, such as Microsoft Xbox 360 and even exported to Flash's SWF format starting in 2012 for a brief period before abandoning further support in early 2013 (Kumparak 2013). Recently Unity announced explicit support for 2D games, including support for a Box2D-style physics engine (Goldstone 2013). The authoring environment for Unity's support for 2D games has a lot in common with the timeline-based authoring tools of Flash, combining code and assets for the authors with a visual interface. Flash authoring tools set a precedent for visual interfaces for game creation tools, despite its not originally being targeted at game creation.

The real legacy of Flash's platformer tutorials is not merely found in the retro and post-retro games the platform enables. The approaches to Flash development and the creation of game mechanics in a system not primarily intended for games would lay the foundation for the "Flash Generation" to create spreadable interactive objects almost as easily as it had created animated memes. Learning to emulate professional game development, even from retro models, empowers creative experimentation. Likewise, the exchange of resources, tutorials, and additional libraries to make this type of game creation easier is at the foundation of the Flash community's model of collaborative knowledge-building and free exchange. This communal approach remains a model for sustainable platforms, particularly for amateur or small team game development, and has even been adopted at the feature level in other game development environments, such as Unity's Asset Store. Flash's innovative approach to authoring left a mark on the innovation and process in platformers, even as it set a standard for learning to program.

Introduction

The strange-looking, monotone yellow alien crashed into a nightmare world, constantly pursued by FBI and other official-looking types trying to end his adventure and possibly his life. The player controls his odds of success primarily by smashing the arrow keys, occasionally shooting or jumping in familiar platformer mechanics. Descended from the same platformer games we examined in the last chapter, *Alien Hominid* (2002) was among the first of many incredibly addictive Flash games, filling the web with an alternative to visiting the arcade or loading up a home console system. The single-player games produced in Flash shaped the boundaries of game aesthetics, popularizing the edgy, typically low-fidelity or intentionally pixelated, high-difficulty and innovative variations on traditional game mechanics that would characterize future entries in the independent games genre. Websites such as Newgrounds transformed the Internet into a successor to the now-mostly-vanished physical arcades, with games that appealed to players who wouldn't necessarily make the investment in long and complex hardcore game experiences or in the expensive dedicated hardware that often went with them, but would nonetheless become a defining part of the new generation of gamers. This had major ramifications for who could play, and when. Downloadable games represent an investment and require a user to have control of their computer: thus, built-in casual games like Windows *Solitaire* and *Minesweeper* were the original refuge of would-be players stuck at work. Juul notes that while preinstalled games, and games requiring installation, contributed to casual gaming, the lowered barrier of entry and investment represented by Flash truly powered an online casual gaming revolution (Juul 2010). The tradition of addictive gameplay for any environment begun with GameBoy's *Tetris* would now overtake both PCs and Macs thanks to the Flash plug-in's status as an essential part of browsing the web.

The Flash platform did not lend itself obviously to the types of games that were dominant on the PC even as Flash games were emerging, and many of the constructions Flash would empower did not look much like "games" at all in comparison to these genres. Long before Flash adopted its first branch, genre conventions were already well defined thanks to the legacy of landmark games from the Atari 2600, the Commodore, and early PC DOS and Windows titles. In the mid-nineties, single-player games, including first-person shooters (FPSs) such as *Quake*, pioneered online gameplay, providing a means of connecting and competing with other players without requiring a browser's intervention. These were heirs to local-area network gameplay, but with multiplayer writ large, using the same protocols and networks that Flash traveled but requiring additional software interpreters beyond a browser and web server to enable the connection. Such games were high-investment, "hardcore" games, which Juul notes as demanding mastery of conventions and standing in polar opposition to the low-investment casual games better suited to Flash (Juul 2010). Both Flash and PC games would further colonize the space between casual and hardcore. For instance, *The Sims*, released by Maxis in 2000, appealed to a different audience than *Zelda* or *Quake*, using a simplified simulation of people's social and consumer activities as the primary game mechanic and followed the original idea of playfulness present in Sid Meier's 1989 *SimCity*. These games provided the first hint that playful interaction may not require the traditional rewards of arcade games, and that culture and creation may be compelling motivations for player involvement in an interactive "toy," not unlike earlier simulation-driven games including *SimCity*. These games sat at the border of casual and hard-core, and introduced many conceptual elements such as aesthetic rewards and social interactions that would recur in later games as the platform grew more sophisticated in its ability to model data-driven environments.

However, these high-investment skills-based games suggested that consoles demanded a lot from their players, helping sustain the stereotype of gamers as mostly adolescent males. The same expectations could be projected on the creators powering Flash games, since the very environment of the Internet was still coupled with an expectation of male technical dominance. This increasing complexity and barriers to entry had an impact on console market share: while navigating *Mario* in two dimensions was relatively easy for newcomers, many gamers abandoned the ongoing skill acquisition (including the new analog pads on the N64 controller) because they simply couldn't keep up with the increasing demand for time and skills. This hard-core tendency among console and PC games was counterbalanced by the rise of casual games, many of which were created using Flash and later became known as "browser-based games" as opposed to "downloadable" due to their instant availability. The image of the player base for these games was quite different, because their accessibility using tools associated with workplace productivity, research, and social networking made them immediately playable for a wide audience. Pivotal titles in this genre included PopCap Games' *Bejeweled*, released in 2001, and more traditional board games such as checkers and chess and even poker. The allure of these games resides in both their large selection and their lack of installation. Users spend large amounts of time in their browsers, whether while chatting, working, searching, or browsing. Flash provided many of the core gameplay and subjects that occurred in longer-form games but at a much more accessible level of time commitment. These games still required infrastructure to reach the wider audiences. Newgrounds grew slowly from its initial capacities to support the increased demand for bandwidth, forcing the site to seek funding through advertisements in 1999 (Fulp 1999).

The very concept of games that pass through networks with the same speed as viral videos or memes opened up a world of possibilities for short, experimental, often quirky games from independent or first-time game makers. These games wove themselves into the social fabric of the web, providing outlets for procrastination and play. On the other side of the social spectrum, a number of games have used Flash to exploit the new possibilities for multiplayer as enabled by web platforms. Nearly everyone on Facebook—even those who strongly identify as non-gamers—has been exposed to Zynga's 2009 release *FarmVille*, which debuted as a Flash game where the player was enticed to cultivate crops and translate social capital into game capital using contacts on Facebook. The undeniable economic success of these types of social games changed the expectations of asynchronous gameplay and gameplay that subsists on social platforms. The unique combination of the emergence of the Facebook platform and the close integration with Flash's web capabilities led to a rush of interest by developers first in the social network space and later in the extended space of mobile games that were connected to social network accounts. Such experiments also offered new models for profiting from web games through micropayments to further extend and customize gameplay. Elsewhere, experiments with multiplayer were much more demanding: AOL and later other gaming portals provided players with communities and subscriptions to game clients that didn't even have single-player modes, but that charged an hourly (and later a monthly) fee for access to the servers that they ran on. These games were essentially PC games that launched and connected to central servers for real-time interaction with other players. The launch of *EverQuest* in 1999, following in the tradition of *Ultima Online*, brought about the next step in this model by asking for a flat monthly subscription to a single 3D PC game that took massive investments of time and skill to advance in (and develop). These persistent worlds have in some cases continued for years, thanks in part to the willingness of their players to address substantial time and identity into the space. As Flash games have matured, persistent real-time MMOs have been released using the technology, including *AdventureQuest Worlds* by Artix Entertainment, LLC in 2008.

However, Flash games could also use the benefits of web distribution to go where other game platforms might fear to tread. Along with the indie games and the larger companies' explorations, the Internet's anonymity and typical demographics led to a profusion of adult content expressed in Flash's medium. Adult-oriented interactive Flash movies and games were hosted and popularized on the very same portals as indie games, and as such they provide a productive lens into the communities that both view and create them. The games range from the simple, minimally interactive to more elaborate romantic-style games and outright pornographic content. Such games at the fringes of Flash offer a potent reminder of what can happen on a platform whose creator has chosen not to act as a content regulator, but instead to let absolutely anyone create content for Flash. This openness shaped all of Flash's genres. In this chapter we'll examine Flash's impact on the various casual games on the web. Flash's inviting, colorful aesthetics and near universally available format positioned it as the ideal platform for pioneering examples of various casual genres. The popularity and success of these genres were magnified by the networked context of Flash games, taking advantage of a community of sharing and criticism (such as Newgrounds) or communities originally built around various social connections (Facebook). Creators, both amateur and increasingly corporate, have realized the potential of Flash to tap into player's interstitial time and leverage the persistent state and to find the intersection of behavioral economics and behavioral psychology through these communities' willing participation.

Figure 4.1
Alien Hominid, 2002, Tom Fulp

Indie Games

In 2002, Newgrounds founder Tom Fulp released a throwback Flash game featuring an alien trying to survive his crash landing on Earth in a side-scrolling battle against the FBI, as shown in figure 4.1. The game's graphics and simple animation were not unlike the amateur works of Flashimation that were still prominent on Newgrounds, but it stood as an impressive example of Flash's potential for independent game development at a time when "indie" (independent) was still an emerging concept in gaming. In its ten years on Newgrounds, the free version of *Alien Hominid* has been played twenty million times (Hinkle 2012).

Flash's previously demonstrated potential as an amateur tool for game creation was finally being unlocked. This was thanks in part to advancements in Flash itself that allowed creators to move past the timeline-jumping strategy of the first Flash pinball game to more complex interactivity and user-controlled systems. In the last chapter we discussed the key components to platformers, collision detection and simple object-based scripting. The next most useful feature was external code and libraries, so that redundant tasks could be reused in future games. These libraries ranged from physics (such as Box2D) to common game organization and tasks (Flixel). In the hands of new developers sharing their knowledge, Flash's features that supported gaming were being mastered, recorded, and compartmentalized to allow for an even lower barrier of entry to development.

But first, games like *Alien Hominid*'s retro game style and recreation of a classic console platformer experience through the lens of Flash demonstrated what amateur creators could achieve, and played a part in making Newgrounds an enduring Flash arcade that truly showcases "Everything. By Everyone"—as the site's most recent tagline promises. The inclusiveness in the community's motto promised an exciting future for Flash, the chosen development tool for much of the "everything" being released. The community still features prominent advice boards for exchanging knowledge as well as the primary showcase of completed projects, and many queries center on accomplishing certain tricks of animation or game development in Flash.

When Flash first emerged as a tool for game making in the early 2000s, the games found on the site, including the 16-bit graphical feel of *Alien Hominid* itself, didn't look much like the rest of contemporary gaming. If anything, it looked like a step backward, as ports of traditional console games and arcade classics examined previously reflect. But this wasn't just a development limitation: these games filled a different space than their contemporaries, and were shaped by their dependence on the browser for access and distribution. The lack of controller was only the beginning of the distinction from the gaming world where *Alien Hominid* landed. The history of gaming at the turn of the millennium holds many major milestones, including the release of Sony's PlayStation 2, Nintendo's GameCube, and Microsoft's Xbox, a trio of consoles that promised to outshine any Flash game with their sheer technical might. By this point, consoles had settled on customized controllers with dedicated thumbsticks and sported high-powered graphics cards, although Nintendo would choose smaller more efficient platforms than its rivals. While the PC held its own as a platform thanks to both native genres (including the massively multiplayer online role-playing game, which had continued to evolve since the release of *Ultima Online*) and ports of console games, hard-core gaming power appeared to be settling into the living room. Personal computers were becoming more common than ever before, reaching over 50 percent of U.S. households according to the 2000 census (New York Times 2001). These new PC users were still figuring out what else to use their home computer for. Unlike the expensive investment of consoles, or even the CD-ROM-based, long-form games made for PC, Flash games could easily be played on any home, work, or school computer with a browser and Internet connection. This accessibility combined with speed of play and diversity of content would allow Flash games to reach beyond the market of "gamers" to introduce many to the idea of gameplay on the Internet. Through the same portals for amateur-developed projects that characterized Flashimation, *Alien Hominid* brought new players to Newgrounds, even after it became a console game.

At the time of Flash 5's release by Macromedia in 2000, the term "games" was nowhere to be found in either the description of the software's capabilities or the review by Macworld (Heid 2000). This omission indicated that Macromedia had little idea of the future developments that would follow. The choice of a label of a platform directly communicates its purpose and those of its user-developers. Adobe's website for Flash as of August 2012 contained the following description: "Game developers around the world use Flash. See their work at gaming.adobe.com" (Adobe 2012). The slogan for Adobe Gaming now closely echoes the Newgrounds slogan: "Better games. More easily. For more people" (Adobe 2012). Flash in 2000 was marketed as providing access to an interactive media format, keeping in mind use cases that focused on common website goals like providing access to information using animation and multimedia. Just as the evolution of Flash animation pushed the platform beyond banner ad–like movements, reminiscent of GIFs, that FutureSplash's marketing originally suggested, the evolution of Flash games would create demands for sophistication in the client's capabilities as well as access to those features through authoring tools to utilize them. These two uses would in turn underlie one of the fundamental tensions of the platform, as Flash sought to accommodate both users looking to create the simple interactive experiences it was originally designed to convey and power users who sought ever-more-sophisticated web possibilities. Much of the future overcomplication of the toolset and the strange disconnect between the Timeline's historical model of animation and the scripting language can be laid to rest on this duality.

Flash games came about as amateur creators realized how similar the capabilities were to older game platforms, while at the same time being far more accessible. These creators included Jonathan Gay and many others who published on Newgrounds. While PC games were always on the cutting edge of using game-related hardware such as faster CPUs and dedicated video cards, Flash met the basic requirements for interactive gameplay: display of color graphics synced to sound and capacity to handle user input, in the form of mouse input and keyboard. Flash games were in many cases self-published and independently developed without a budget, which went hand in hand with the platform's original purpose. Indie game development outside of Flash was a more expensive proposition. Consoles like the Wii and Xbox required developers to purchase hardware development kits and license expensive software development kits, in addition to providing fees to distribute the game itself. Each console had its own graphical limitations and controller layouts, providing additional obstacles to independent developers creating games for multiple platforms. Flash, on the other hand, was developed using a single software package at the time and had no licensing fees. In addition, all Flash games assumed what computers already had—a mouse, a keyboard, and a monitor—this schema that would lend itself to certain interfaces that would gradually dominate PC gaming thanks to the combination of browser-based and installed games. For instance, the use of arrow keys to substitute for an arcade or console game's control pad as a movement schema is seen in every platformer imitation discussed in the previous chapter, as well as in most of the casual games under examination here.

In part thanks to these limitations, Flash lent itself to different types of interactions than other popular gaming platforms of the time, while reaching an audience of non-gamers whose expectations were shaped by Flash's controls rather than console hardware. While hardcore PC gaming took advantage of the latest joysticks and game controllers, focusing more on 3D navigation and environments, Flash creators were left free to explore as-yet-unrealized potentials of 2D gameplay. Likewise, console game evolution followed a linear, almost mythical ascent across spatial dimensions, Flash spread out to colonize each possible core action that the player takes to move the game forward, also known as a game mechanic, that could be realized using simple mouse and keyboard input. In *Alien Hominid*, that characteristic controller style replaces a console's keypad, with the user relying on arrow keys to move and letters to shoot. The constraint of not having access to specialized controllers or hardware forced developers seeking to use Flash to develop "usable" games—games that could be played immediately by most computer users who often had Flash already installed. This independence from any peripheral devices is part of the allure of these games, playable as a diversion at any time and from any computer, allowing the games to invade both work and school as quick breaks in the same way that various editions of Microsoft Window's bundled *Solitaire* allows. The games and patterns that began in the early 2000s would lead to the pervasive social games that were produced by Zynga later in the decade using Flash, including *FarmVille* and *Words with Friends*.

Another key difference between Flash and PC titles was the fact that most games were free. The communal focus of free content exchange that Flash communities represent is part of a larger trend that David Bollier terms the "viral spiral." He describes the evolution of code into social platforms: "The viral spiral began with free software (code that is free to use, not code at no cost) and later produced the Web. Once these open platforms had sufficiently matured, tech wizards realized that software's greatest promise is not as a stand-alone tool on PCs, but as a social platform for Web-based sharing and collaboration" (Bollier 2008). Alternative tools to create Flash content would not be freely available until Adobe took over the reins and made compilers available. But even given the price of admission to creating Flash games, the alternative—learning a low-level language like C and then developing a game engine or buying a premade game engine—was also expensive, both in time and in money. We go further into the implications of Adobe's choices with regards to opening parts of the platform in chapter 6. Low barriers to procedural literacy and a wealth of community support pushed the casual game revolution into motion as part of that "viral software," even though a legal, licensed copy of the Flash authoring tool was a relatively high barrier to entry—a cost that further determined the demographics of Flash creators.

Free, in the monetary sense, also dictated the rituals required to gain admission to creating Flash games: the early days of Flash consisted of constant re-creation of implementation ideas from scratch. Each mechanic employed in a Flash game, however common, had no single game engine to draw from. Instead, the affordances of the Flash software platform became a highly constrained game development environment that favored certain game mechanics over others and prevented the transmission of knowledge from one game to the next. This limitation would later be addressed by game libraries such as Flixel, an open source game engine foundation following the philosophy of shared resources noted as essential to encouraging Bollier's viral spiral. However, until those resources were shared and collaborative, each author who wanted to manage fundamental game mechanics such as collisions or dialogue by necessity had to invent their own solution. Flash did not inherently provide a coding base for these shared challenges, a challenge that the community would have to address.

Even though the games were free to players, the bandwidth and the costs of hosting required to provide them were not. The same models that supported previous Flash content and even web portals came into play, including ads and banners. The same portals that were hosting animated shorts began to add interactive movies, most catering to tastes that lay outside the mainstream animation. Games came to be united with animations under the description of "Flash," further strengthening the tie to the technology's signature characteristics of vector animation, interactivity, and amateur authorship. The recognizable crowdsourced models of sites such as the flagship Newgrounds allowed for recognition of quality to be equally based upon recognition by fellow amateurs, with the common framework of Flash uniting their creative output. In 2000, Newgrounds became the first Flash portal to automate its submission process. Instead of sorting through each submission and making decisions, Fulp and Ross Snyder made plans to automate the process. Users could then vote down submissions enough that they would be "blammed" or removed. This system resembled other ventures that began noncommercially, including Slashdot and Wikipedia. Unlike gaming consoles, whose brand was essential in drawing audiences to purchase the hardware to play their exclusive content, Flash did not have a clear identity as a game platform. Macromedia never sought to sell Flash as a brand to users. They marketed Flash to developers directly who in turn sought to promote the technology in a haphazard, crowdsourced way even as players and distributors recognized the platform's utility. These communal portals blurred the lines between developer and user, because ultimately full participation included content creation. While a hierarchy of skill and success certainly developed within these communities, they continued to encourage ascension by new user-developers, and Newgrounds continues to host contests for new Flash animation and games judged by veterans from within the community.

Given this tradition of amateur production, most early Flash games were created without budgets to reside on sites that were monetized via ads and merchandise. A common profit model included releasing a demo version to a site like Newgrounds, and then requiring a purchase to obtain the full version. Because of the relatively unsecured nature of SWFs, these purchased files were often posted on file sharing websites, not even requiring a "crack." Thus while major portal sites and their creators could profit on the ads revenue produced by hosting Flash games, the creators themselves rarely benefitted in financial rewards. Instead, sharing their work offered the chance to gain a reputation and notoriety, perhaps even leading to a coveted featured spot on the portal's main page, making it more likely that their work would be visible to the rest of the community.

These communities continued to be driven by amateur creativity. The humor and sensibilities of early Flash games were decidedly adolescent, perhaps reflecting the role of students in driving content creation (the college students who founded the site aged but stayed with the project, continuing to run the community). The same places that brought amateur work to a larger audience also met the needs for tutorials, information, and examples to enable them to do so. Users who joined Newgrounds as viewers rather than developers were still part of the discourse of creation, offering critiques and suggestions and elevating the works through their exchanges. The relatively few requirements to create a work viewed by hundreds or thousands colored the content as well as the quality. Many works swing between parody and commentary, the hyper-violent and overtly adult. Designing and producing a console or PC game was out of reach for many without a background in 3D or computer programming, but the desire to create games was not, leading to experimentation and imitation in the more accessible confines of the Flash platform. This combination produced a whole array of fan-driven works, games that either drew from a single aspect of another game or that borrowed characters, plots, and even assets (as in the case of *Mario* games, or other classic games as discussed in a previous chapter). These games coexisted with fan-made animations.

One of the earliest works of complexity that came just before Flash 5's release was a point-and-click shooter called *Pico's School* (figure 4.2)

Figure 4.2
Pico's School, 2006, Tom Fulp

developed by Newgrounds creator Tom Fulp in 1999. The piece was rer-eleased in 2006 and currently has over six million views. It helped launch Newgrounds as a public force while highlighting some of the culture that would be synonymous with the portal through its blend of darkness and humor with inspiration from the Columbine high school shooting. The player takes on the role of a student whose classmates are killed by a group of stereotypical goth students. As the player battles those students, Pico learns that they are actually ninjas and aliens. The game is filled with both the surrealism and toilet humor that often characterizes the Newgrounds community: a pack of weed serves as a health potion and a kid throws excrement from a toilet stall. It was hailed by many as the pinnacle of Flash 3 "programming," and it offered a first model for the type of point-and-click interactivity that would become a standard. Developer Tom Fulp admitted that the structure of the game's code was heavily influenced by the Flash format at the time: "Pico was made in Flash 3, before the avail-ability of variables (or just about any code, for that matter). To simulate stored data, I weaved a complex web of movie clips that gave orders to the main game" (Fulp 1999). Sections of movieclips were labeled with numbers, and the game constantly jumped from reference point to refer-ence point based on player actions—a mechanic that created considerable strain during highly interactive moments like a final boss fight with a swastika-blasting alien Cassandra. Works such as this one were heralded for the technical innovation that pushed others within the community to try to accomplish even more under the same systemic constraints. Pushing the Flash platform beyond its envisioned potential became part of the amateur developer community's own metagame, with accolades within the community reserved for victors.

The Rise of ActionScript

The release of Flash 5 coincided with a large change in the authoring of Flash: ActionScript was now a language, and as such it could be attached to MovieClips, frames, and sprites. The syntax also changed drastically, moving from the custom set of commands that are closer to the specifica-tion to a more standardized language, ECMAScript. The slash syntax remained, at least at first, as would the toolbox option (and some form of it would persist until even the current version, Adobe Flash Creative Cloud). As we discussed in the last chapter, many programmers encoun-tered Flash as a first programming environment after transitioning from the markup syntax of traditional web development. But Flash 5 was now recognizable even to developers bringing expectations from C or Java: a few key elements, common in other programming languages, emerged including parameterized function calls and local variables. These features are particularly relevant to games, since games in a given genre often share a great deal of functionality. Flash 5 also acknowledged the needs of programmers by including its first debugger, which allows programmers to see and change property values as the work plays.

Along with these changes to the language, ActionScript was freed from the editor into its own file extension, ".as." This enables libraries to be shared and used across multiple projects, though Flash projects would not be fully compatible with version control systems until much later. Previously the demands of interactive gameplay required developers to provide directions reminiscent of assembly language or at least BASIC, resplendent with a programmer's nightmare: a spaghetti of GOTO statements and lack of higher-level organization or abstraction. Now developers could use the newly introduced classes to store a score with a game object, and even have objects like MovieClips, a display object with frames like a sprite sequence, manage their own states or handle collisions.

This made it possible for creators with little more than desire and images on the Internet to follow a tutorial such as the ones found on Flash Kit, another Flash development community web site (Doull 2001). Once a developer learned how to track the user's clicks, handle arrow key presses, and understand the basics of collisions, an amateur user would be capable of creating a fully functioning (yet simple) Flash game. Before, such feats considerably stretched the original intent of the system. Now, the environment corresponded more directly with the extension of Flash's capabilities by users seeking even greater interactivity in web production. In particular, assigning loops and using classes made frame references a lot more readable (and in many cases unnecessary). The creators of a platform aren't always aware of the best uses for it, or even how to teach others to use it. Thus the role of user-developers was particularly important to the evolution of Flash as a platform, and was one reason why Macromedia and later Adobe relied on their developers for examples, tutorials, and eventually maintenance of part of the system itself. Creators seeking to build better games were particularly driven to push at the platform's limitations, as it provided the access to players but did not inherently cater to their needs as game designers. Thanks to the same drive to experiment that drove the first Flash pinball game, pioneers of web-based gaming genres took advantage of new tools to demonstrate Flash's potential to create meaningful play. Online gaming was one of those experiments that would lead to a full genre for which Flash was well positioned.

Flash Games

The term "Flash game" is closely associated with casual gaming, and many of the prejudices and discussions relating to casual gaming are mapped and directed likewise at Flash as the enabling platform. PC games have inherited their name and distinction in opposition to console games, indicating that they can be played on any number of IBM-compatible systems. The term "browser-based game" only came about when HTML and JavaScript became capable of offering gaming experiences in a similar level of control and interactivity with Flash games. Before that, "Flash games" took on the connotations of "Free," "variable quality," and "addictive." The last is particularly noteworthy as addictiveness is used as a positive feature in a browser game. This means that the games and some combination of gameplay, persistence (in some cases), and availability stick in ways that games such as chess or checkers do not.

Flash games connote a shortened form, and thus promise a potential for novelty that more extensive games might not. The novelty is driven by the sheer potential in surrounding content: Flash games incorporate virtually everything discussed or mentioned on the web, from popular memes to philosophical reflections. Inside the often cloned and many times verified game mechanics, other game mechanics were finding realization, the community around which they were praised and taught to embrace countercultural games and narrative experiences. This continual reinvention allows for clarification of the stickiness of Flash game's forms, even as the forms were continually morphed to meet the needs of the latest pop culture moment. Player's familiarity with the myriad of repeated conventions in Flash games helped make newer forms of games acceptable because they were based on experiences and threads that were already understood. The concept of bite-sized and zero-setup games, however, became a hallmark of Flash games. Flash games are also reputed to have several key qualities that Juul describes as essential to being "casual," even if they were not originally designed as such. These include "interruptability," where the game is often too short to have more than the two to six minutes of time required to play it (Juul 2010). Addictive games can be played for much longer periods, relying on complex algorithmic puzzles. Flash games are also accessible, though not in the Human-Computer Interaction (or HCI) usage of that term, by virtue of the simplicity in tools both to create and to play the games. The primary use of building-block programming tools means that many Flash games have very similar mechanics, as discussed in the next section. These constraints, while forcing games to focus on a single mechanic, also encourage game developers to adopt a well-known mechanic and to assume players have some experience in it. Instead of games having lengthy tutorial, games have a very experimental or obvious learning curve, where clicking places or just moving the mouse is enough to understand the gist of the game's requests.

Many games we play rely on the simple pleasure of finding patterns. Solitaire, crossword puzzles, and even Sudoku rely on the brain's ability to group, categorize, and otherwise enjoy doing so. Flash games have provided ports of popular physical games, but they have also provided game types that can only be digital. *Bejeweled* has become an emblematic puzzle game on multiple platforms, but it was originally known as the Flash game *Diamond Mine* in 2000. The original game was inspired by the Russian puzzle game *Shariki*, developed for DOS in 1994, whose name, Шáр, is Russian for "The Balls." The genre of match-three games was born from this primordial game.

The player makes a single swap, either vertically or horizontally, and any resulting patterns of three or more blocks of the same color and shape disappear. *Diamond Mine* introduces a means to replenish these empty spaces, making the completion of the level a time-based event instead of exhausting the possible swaps. The programming for the basic game mechanics is simple, consisting of checking after each move whether any set of one or two tiles formed a match, and then if any matches were formed after the tiles settled. The simplicity also gave it an addictive quality; finding patterns was inherently satisfying and the response from the game only added to that satisfaction. Casino games often use similar "juiciness" to provoke players to keep playing.

Bejeweled was a very successful example of the match-three genre. Once the mechanics became familiar enough that it could be grouped in with checkers, the same mechanic was cloned and adapted to a variety of games. The simplicity of the mechanic meant that the game would never be sold for significant money, nor would it justify the expenses of translating to a physical media for a dedicated console. *Puzzle Quest* is one such game that combines the simplicity of the match-three mechanic with a role-playing fiction and ruleset. It would be released first for Nintendo DS and Playstation Portable (PSP) in 2006, then ported to several systems in 2007, including the Wii, PS2, PC, and Xbox Live arcade to critical acclaim (and in some cases, confusion).

But consoles and traditional distribution channels are not the only possibility. Addictive shortform games that award points can also be used as an end in and of themselves, much as Flash portals like Newgrounds use them to attract and keep users. Another alternative, one used by virtual pet social game *Neopets* is to combine the games together into a single system, so that playing one game can yield rewards in the form of art or icons on the site itself. While both systems use advertising, the second uses it in a trademarked way known as "immersive advertisement" where the games themselves are in some cases part of the advertisement. "Advergames," as they are sometimes known, can be either explicit about their status as paid advertisement (above the line) or covert (below the line). They bring the initial idea of adding arcade games to bars back: to attract visitors to spend time in and devote attention to a given place. Promoting commercial brands are one way that these games "stickiness" and ease of use is leveraged. They are a logical application of Flash's characteristic dynamic animation and small footprint, and are exemplified in the semi-interactive banners for which Flash is vilified.

Flash's defining characteristics opened the way for games that would be impossible for traditional publishers to distribute, or games that challenged existing copyrights. These games would engage with fandoms and movie properties such as *The Lord of the Rings* or *Harry Potter*, providing either glimpses into the worlds or outright mockeries of characters and situations. They also included games potentially too crude or explicit to find their way on other platforms.

Erotic Games

Flash's status as both Internet-born technology and the go-to tool of amateurs has made it a particularly active locus for the integration of sex into games and interactive media. Exchange of erotic media had already been active through message boards, newsgroups, and communities such as 4chan. Newgrounds instituted an adult rating for games that were particularly violent or had pornographic content, taking a first step at dealing with communal regulation of content in a community inherently open to experimentation. The genres that deal with erotic subject materials range from the simplistic to the dizzyingly complex, and draw from a mix of sources including Japanese narrative games. Many of these works are created by amateurs, the procedural equivalent of first attempts at passing notes containing illicit drawings in class. The integration of erotic topics such as dating, romance, nudity, and intercourse with arcade games convened on several consistent genres including dating simulations, dress-up games, and intercourse simulation games. These games are not only significant because of their near record number of hits and ratings, but because they, along with games that put forward or challenge political ideologies, represent some of the freedoms that the Flash platform provides compared to a system such as the app store or a console. They are also notable exceptions in a landscape of relative sexless videogames: while characters are sexualized, explicit sex is absent from much of the videogame market, as Tanya Krzywinska (2012) observed in her examination of sex as an often absent game mechanic.

We can directly attribute the exploration of erotic content in Flash game development to the same affordances that make it an apparently open platform, at least as far as content is concerned. (Again, the lack of hardware restrictions and specific dependencies that here separate Flash from hardware platforms makes it a difficult system for any gatekeepers to restrict, freeing it as a medium of exploration.) Unfortunately, much of the freedom Flash grants game developers has been expressed relatively uniformly, taking many attributes of other casual games and mapping them onto content intended for a narrow audience—often demographically assumed to share the same preferences as an overly heterogeneous group of creators, at least within the genre. Most of the games are heteronormative (with a focus on male/female relationships and traditional gender roles) and aesthetically intended to appeal to an imagined male cisgender (referring to those who identify with the sex/gender they were assigned at birth) audience. This reflects the discourse apparent in many of these online communities, as a study of amateur new media communities noted in 2011 after a seven-year study: discrimination and aggression toward women regularly appeared not only in the communities but in the content of the works (Warren, Stoerger, and Kelley 2011). Thus, the use of the Flash platform in many of these instances is socially transgressive but also highly in keeping with the larger inequity in the visible gaming and game development community, which remains skewed toward what Parrott and Zeichner (2003) refer to as the "hypermasculine," or the exaggeration of masculine-gendered appearances and behaviors, usually alongside the degradation of any expression of the feminine. Hypermasculine representations are apparent in the muscular, "Come Get Some" avatars of gaming culture from Duke Nukem to the trench-coated and suited shooting silhouetted men of the Flash game *Ricochet Kills* (2009). Gaming culture at large is rife with hypermasculine stereotypes alongside exaggerated and hypersexualized femininity through a masculine gaze, as Erica Scharrer observed in her study of game marketing (Scharrer 2004). Unsurprisingly, much of the adult content produced with Flash similarly reflects this lens. Flash games thus tend toward the same problems of representation and lack of diversity that is rampant throughout the games industry: while the platform has the potential for subversion, most of the content instead falls into the all-too-familiar.

The distribution of these adult games on the web reflected the practices common with other pornographic media. Flash files were portable and easily copied. Because they could be hosted on any website, many of them were widely shown on portals and game sites (even adult sites) without the original author's permission. This led to a tiered structure and attempts to offer playable "demo" versions of Flash games and full versions, as well as increasingly aggressive ads attached to the beginning of hosted games. Due in part to the viral nature of Flash movie sharing, attempts at generating revenue through direct sales rather than advertisements were not entirely successful. Tools were developed for making return trips to the host site unnecessary, and for many Flash movies, despite their online distribution, they were often played in a stand-alone player or outside of any browser.

Several games focus entirely on sexually explicit activities, in ways no mainstream PC or console game commercially released in the United States can. Characteristics of these games include using motion tweens and meters to indicate different stages of arousal. These representations are well suited to Flash because of their loops, their simple button-based interaction, and their relatively small amount of vector-based content, usually anime-style art. Many of the narrative works that revolve around relationships originated in Japan as ren'ai or romantic simulation games in the 1980s, including the first examples of the mechanics. These games usually center on a heterosexual plot, focusing on either marriage or sexual stimulation. Visual novels are one example of ren'ai where text and static images are used to tell a story. They account for a significant number of narrative works created by amateurs in Flash, often using anime-styled visuals. Visual novels don't have very many branches, and usually no number or statistic tracking, as is characteristic of dating simulations (or sims) that rely on numbers more than branching narratives. Despite being relatively shallow compared to interactive dramas, romance games elicit a particularly strong emotional investment and attention from netizens. The proof lies in how the top-visited game on Newgrounds is not an addictive puzzle game or a violent adolescent affair, but rather a "gamified," simplistic, and even offensive representation of dating multiple partners. The mechanics that drive the game involve quizzes and memory tests, as well as an inventory system similar to the conventions of point-and-click adventure games.

SIMGIRLS is a stat-based dating simulator that acquired over forty-eight million views in the decade plus since its initial release in 2002, and it is known—even if not played—by the same generation that made *Homestar Runner* and *Alien Hominid* hits. In the Newgrounds community history, the game is noted for launching a craze of successors: "Like a Pandora's Box that perhaps shouldn't have been opened, Hentai Simgirls started the dating game craze on Newgrounds" (Fulp 2013b). The game is best recognized as an example of *bishojo*, a subgenre of erotic games focusing on "interactions with beautiful girls" (Galbraith 2011). SIMGIRLS in particular focuses on a teenage boy navigating high school in an unremarkable way until a girl from the future alters his DNA and accidentally makes him a "megaplayboy." The player then moves through relationships with different girls using the character's new charm. The gender dynamics are strongly focused on the eventual submission of the girls (including the girl from the future, who ends up living in his basement as a "pet"); the creator, "sim-man," has continued to expand the project, adding "tons of new really hardcore hentai scenes" as of Version 5.0 (sim-man 2002). The result remains, according to the Newgrounds wiki, the most viewed submission of any kind in the community's history. While the genre of *bishojo* began on consoles as a huge industry in Japan, the proliferation of these games into online spaces brought them into international popular culture. This is only possible because of the lax or nonexistent content regulation both in Flash as a platform and communities such as Newgrounds. Such games can easily be banned in closed platforms. For instance, Apple has aggressively policed similar content, using both ratings and ambiguously enforced policies to prevent similar material from appearing on top app lists or in the press (Stoneback 2009). These policies are reminiscent of Nintendo's seal of quality and are seen by some as a positive step forward for the balancing act of protection versus censorship (Martinelli 2009). The decision made early on by Macromedia to freely distribute Flash Player without restrictions on its use allowed this content to exist and to be easily accessed.

Amateur game creation far exceeded the output of any other platforms, including Processing and C/C++. It became a voice for fan-based works and through silly games helped achieve a critical mass of procedural literacy, the likes of which had first been seen in the adventure gaming and interactive fiction communities. Flash was an attractive language to learn because of its use in popular games, and it was often recommended as a first language, capable of producing satisfying reactions in a short period and pursued by adolescents motivated by their favorite Newgrounds hits.

Social Network Games

Games were not the first love for Flash or its authors, but the relationship that came about formed expectations for casual gaming for years to come.

Distribution channels took full advantage of the nature of Flash files that were discrete, self-contained, and able to be fit into uniform slots in database-driven web portals. Even then, such portals provided programmatic access from the game to the context of the community that hosted it. From achievements to high scores, these integrations set the stage for a whole new genre of games that used a social network for its spread and as a core aspect of its game mechanic. With the persistent game and timer-based mechanics along with bite-sized gameplay sessions, the stage was set for the mobile revolution. The same models of use and distribution would popularize free-to-play as a primary economic model and standardize casual gameplay in similarly calibrated iPad and iPhone applications.

The economics of Flash games would mature when Zynga's flagship games, including *FarmVille*, raked in extraordinary revenue, inviting criticism and emulation across the games industry. Chris Lewis explores the reasoning behind the success in light of behavioral theories for design patterns through the lens of behavioral economics (Lewis, Wardrip-Fruin, and Whitehead 2012). Lewis describes how similar strategies are used in games with very different audiences and mechanics. The social integration of *FarmVille* is perhaps the best answer to the question of its popularity, as A. J. Patrick Liszkiewicz noted in a talk on *FarmVille*'s repetitive, labor-intense mechanics: "Again: if *Farmville* is laborious to play and aesthetically boring, why are so many people playing it? The answer is disarmingly simple: *people are playing Farmville because people are playing Farmville*" (Liszkiewicz 2010). The concept of a social game as one persists through social networks owes a debt to earlier SWF files and how they traveled virally, except instead of single files being hosted and repurposed by multiple portals, each user in a social network becomes a producer and marketing channel that advertises and distributes multiple "social games," enticing through news feeds and other means their network and publishing their status or achievements in the game.

FarmVille and other Ville-style games capitalize on several characteristics of Flash, including its ease of being closely integrated with a social network's API. Game developers have variously attempted to explain and understand the phenomena. One developer, Ian Bogost, created a game to distill the game mechanics to their absurd minimalist interpretation in a social network game called *Cow Clicker*. In it, the entire purpose of the game is to accumulate the most clicks, which are executed on a timer, much as many game mechanics in other social network games. The game's description is explicit at its goals, even though it has far outstretched them:

Cow Clicker is a Facebook game about Facebook games. It's partly a satire, and partly a playable theory of today's social games, and partly an earnest example of that genre.

You get a cow. You can click on it. In six hours, you can click it again. Clicking earns you clicks. You can buy custom "premium" cows through micropayments (the Cow Clicker currency is called "mooney"), and you can buy your way out of the time delay by spending it. You can publish feed stories about clicking your cow, and you can click friends' cow clicks in their feed stories. Cow Clicker is Facebook games distilled to their essence. (Bogost 2010)

Creating a social game is not necessarily easy using the authoring interface; the creation requires a combination of networking and careful design. Facebook games must integrate into the site in a very specific way, and must also consistently adapt to changes in its API. Social games are thus positioned at a highly unstable technical intersection between the Facebook API and the capabilities of Flash Player. Most web-based APIs have adopted the standard REST framework, which the Flash API does not support natively. Another important standard that Flash games required was the OAuth and OAuth 2.0 protocols. These protocols negotiated the sensitive privacy of the Facebook platform by guaranteeing both that the player was who they identified themselves as and that the application had permission to access the user's data, including the ever important wall and contacts list.

These technical challenges were eased, at least in part, by a number of libraries and support. Before Facebook introduced its separate gaming APIs, it provided links to libraries to ease these basic tasks. These libraries could be updated by the creators, and many were maintained as open source projects. They effectively reduced the amount of maintenance required by Facebook developers, but didn't do so entirely. Bogost recounts this relationship between Facebook developers and Facebook as highly problematic in his own experience developing *Cow Clicker*:

Facebook's systems are cobbled together in a way that helps Facebook accomplish its goals. Those include rapid changes proffering near-real-time results, thus producing familiar but slightly altered ongoing attention on the part of its users, of which its developers are a subset. But there's another aspect of rapid, reckless change that few discuss: it helps create a sense of confusion and desperation that forces developers to devote more and more attention to the Facebook Platform. What better way to increase collective commitment to Facebook apps than to quietly extort incremental time out of its creators, time that might otherwise be committed to competing products or—gasp—to their own businesses or personal lives? (Bogost 2013)

His observations were that the Facebook platform evolved more than any single library could handle, that deep changes such as Facebook's release of its Graph API and subsequent Graph Search were in fact a form of lock-in for developers to constantly keep their applications up to date. Adobe Flex attempted to homogenize many of these access protocols, but the exact API could never be properly abstracted, especially because new features and requirements would necessitate wide-ranging changes to an applications structure. In contrast, the Flash API was relatively steady, with its backward compatibility keeping the former ActionScript Virtual Machine (AVM) even as it introduced the more efficient version so that sites running on ActionScript 2 would not fail.

Social games have had an indelible impact on the audience and the nature of online gaming. Game developers who have traditionally developed more traditional titles have also created games in the genre, including John Romero's *Ravenwood Fair*. Flash's role in their genesis and their continued presence on platforms such as Facebook result from the attractive audience and viral participation, the ease of authoring afforded by Flash, and the ready availability of tutorials and gaming libraries. The overall aesthetic of the platform has also worked its way into the DNA of social network games, including vector-based graphics and saturated color palettes. Flash's primary strengths also contributed to the evolution of some of the more nefarious behaviors used in casual and social games, as its instant-on availability quickly gave rise to more intermittent, timer-based gameplay mechanics that are often used to entice and retain player attention through multiple play sessions. Social games have often stood in opposition to indie games, owing not only to their higher entry requirements (large servers and even larger amounts of content required) but to their desire to be independent and artistic. Bogost describes the artistic possibilities of social games as "shit crayons," where humanity can fashion artistic achievements in spite of the limitations imposed by a given circumstance (Bogost 2011a).

Conclusion

Despite the casual and social names attached to games born from Flash, the impact of the platform has principally been through innovating distribution channels and exploding genres into single, bite-sized, and therefore casual pieces. The flexibility of both the authoring tools and the lack of a single authority controlling content gave way to both culturally innovative and completely droll contributions in staggering quantities. The needs of a gaming platform, though not originally the focus of the technology, became the driving force behind future developments in the API and the Flash runtime. 3D graphics were first brought by ambitious programmers to Flash by repurposing techniques derived from developing for decades-old consoles. These concepts successfully thrived in the resource-constrained sandboxed plug-ins that Flash ran in, and the result was unexpectedly striking aesthetics for web-based graphics.

These innovations and this broad appeal have had a lasting effect on casual gaming and PC gaming as a whole, reflected both in critical venues and in the collective memory of our first experiences browsing the net while bored in grade school. Flash earned its identity as a medium and not just a platform, representing the untamed edge of Internet interests and creativity. It attained the love of the masses, proudly proclaimed and exonerated with the same passion as its execution is currently being demanded. Flash can be seen as a prototyping tool and as an end in itself, but its trajectory as a game platform is marked by one-offs, several shooting stars, and an army of clones. The significance of creating these games even when the work is fundamentally derivative or possibly unplayable holds echoes of Lessig's thoughts on communities of remixers whose "showing is valuable, even when the stuff produced is not" (Lessig 2008, 77). When Flash creators are viewed as participating in this type of community, the platform's games can be viewed as providing a trajectory of influence that has fundamentally reshaped expectations for gaming on any device. Even as Flash is diminished as a game development tool by the new cross-platform demands of mobile phones and tablets, this legacy of pervasive, immediately playable games that appeal to a wide-ranging audience can be seen in everything from *Angry Birds* to *Plants vs. Zombies*.

Alien Hominid blasted onto the indie scene as the first example of a Flash game making the leap from browser-based games to consoles. Despite the love affair with Flash, its creators, Tom Fulp and Dan Paladin, sought the more traditional console market to realize their vision for the game. Fulp and Paladin updated the game, both in platform and in content, as a new independent videogame company called the Behemoth. Once rewritten for consoles, *Alien Hominid* won awards at the Independent Games Festival and was a finalist at IndieCade's predecessor, Slamdance 2005. The lines between the "prototype," as the Flash version became known, and the success of the more advanced console version, are blurred by shared concepts and aesthetics. This transformation is a testament to the power of Flash in empowering truly independent game development with lasting results for the industry. Using Flash as a tool to develop a game avoids many of the pitfalls facing independent game developers, including licensing fees associated with console development kits, the complexities of acquiring or building a game engine for the desired console, and later fees associated with online distribution channels like Stream, Xbox live Arcade, and now Apple's app store. Flash and games cannot now be separated.

Introduction

The image of an industrial building fills the browser window. A sculpture, Auguste Rodin's Inferno-inspired *The Gates of Hell*, stands on one side of the interior across from a stack of nine refrigerators. Figures stand in a doorway in front of the gallery label "Young-Hae Chang Heavy Industries/ Bust Down the Door!" while red text fills the screen, flashing quickly as rhythmic words and music pounds through the speakers. Messages emerge almost too fast to be processed: "He busts down the door while I sleep, rushes into my home, enters my bedroom, drags me out of bed, pushes me in my underwear out into the street" (Young-Hae Chang Heavy Industries 2000). This 2004 Flash piece is a remix of the team's 2000 "Bust Down the Doors!," a work of Flash art originally displayed on the networked refrigerators pictured at the Samsung Museum of Art in Seoul. As the artists, Young-Hae Chang and Marc Voge, explained: "Advertisers would have us believe that the Internet refrigerator puts the housewife at the cutting-edge of modern, hi-tech life. We titled our piece *The Gates of Hell* because, on the contrary, we feel that their refrigerator helps keep women in the kitchen" (Tribe 2007b). Mark Tribe describes the work as taking advantage of Flash's "basic features: how to make text appear on the screen and how to set an animation to music. Like Nam June Paik discovering video, a form that would define his artistic practice, Chang and Voge had found their medium." In the hands of Chang and Voge, Flash moved from the gallery and back to the web. Flash's inherent mobility from display spaces to the browser allows the digital to coexist with the physicality of the artists' work: an expressive affordance not necessarily intended in Flash, but perceived and capitalized on by the artists.

Chang and Voge worked within the Flash platform's fundamental strengths, taking some of the Flash aesthetic as fuel for their own style, as John Zuern noted in his study of their 2002 piece *Dakota*. Dakota opens with a minimalist series of blank screens: "Viewed within the context of the Flash environment, these opening screens can be seen to contain another allusion—to the 'loading sequences' that introduce any number of Flash productions currently on the Internet. These often comprise a simple animation that offers some indicator, frequently a progress bar or the word 'loading,' that runs until enough of the opening frames of the movie have been downloaded to the reader's computer to begin playing without stalls" (Zuern 2003). Zuern describes these as choices of optimization that become part of the poetics of the text: such loading screens are primarily intended to prevent the viewer from seeing the unfinished resources assemble themselves on the screen as the computer downloads materials from the server, but in this context they further call attention to how the text is constructed. Some of the same poetics are apparent in *Bust Down the Door*, which as a remix of an earlier work is already embracing one of Flash's primary attributes: its endlessly rearrangeable materiality, within which assets and timelines could be altered to produce a work both new and old. Such remixed works are self-consciously digital, aware of their mechanisms and drawing attention to the interaction not just between art object and viewer but between computer and server. Jessica Pressman refers to the work of Chang and Voge as part of "digital modernism," characterized by taking concepts of modernism and "remediating them in Flash" (Pressman 2009, 318). Pressman notes how the aesthetics of Flash work in favor of that remediation by allowing for a "tension between the visible and the obfuscated, the legible and the illegible, at the levels both of the screen and the code" thanks to Flash's file format's compiled and inaccessible state (2009, 319). Moreover, Pressman's study of Chang and Voge's work highlights the Flash platform's suitability to the work she views ad digital modernism, where even the choices the artist makes about which features and interactive possibilities in Flash to utilize work in tension with a viewer's traditional expectations of software and web applications.

Even as these artists were experimenting with Flash's underlying materiality, those same properties were being redefined. 2004 also saw the introduction of Flash MX 2004 and with it new ActionScript capabilities: as one columnist wrote at the time, "in just under seven years,

Macromedia had matured Flash from simple animation to a full-featured, sophisticated tool you can use to develop rich, multimedia solutions for the web" (David 2003). These new affordances would help usher in more complex experiments with Flash as a platform for interactive art, a category that exists alongside and in parallel to gaming and animation, drawing on Flash's tools for both. Another team of artists profiled by Mark Tribe, Mendi and Keith Obadike, were making use of this interactivity through their 2003 Flash game *Fox Hunt*. The game appeared as part of a larger project, *The Pink of Stealth*, exploring a racially and class-charged romance of sorts between two characters (Tribe 2007b). The game is a fairly simple chase of a fox by a hunter based on an Oscar Wilde quote: "The unspeakable in full pursuit of the uneatable." Points are earned for being "uneatable" or "unspeakable." The work was part of a series the artist explained as "a suite of Internet works intended to explore the language of color and its relationship to art, the body, and politics . . . as a new kind of media-based public performance" (Obadike and Obadike 2006). Previous works in the series were even more staged for unexpected public spaces (as with an auction of "blackness" on eBay, which was ultimately shut down by the site). This further illuminates the potential of digital modernism, and of new media art as an invasion that increases our awareness of the structures and expectations of the web around us.

Reena Jana and Mark Tribe draw attention to this role of the Internet in moving these experiments outside the gallery space: "For many New Media artists, the Internet is not only a medium but also an arena in which to intervene artistically: an accessible public space similar to an urban sidewalk or square where people converse, do business, or just wander around. Part of the appeal of this space is that it is outside the museum-gallery complex, and thus gives artists access to a broad, non-art audience" (Jana and Tribe 2006). By co-opting the same tools as commercial productions, new media Flash artists were particularly able to interrupt expected online discourse. Flash was already ubiquitous online as a tool of marketing: Flash banner ads are both as commonplace and disliked on the Internet as are billboards and animated advertisements on highways and street corners, and are some of Flash's more omnipresent commercial artifacts. Flash has also been applied to the more holistic advertising strategy of marketing through artistic persuasive websites. The appeal of such an apparently neutral, yet contested and well-traveled space recalls the lack of gatekeepers cited by animation artists as part of their motivation for colonizing the web space. Despite this positioning of Flash as a platform for interactive art aimed at a "non-art" audience, most of the early examples from new media art's attempt to define the nebulous category of emerging web art are installations or hypertext. But the diversity of works possible on the platform makes Flash technology a visible part of a range of curated experiences, from art shows to film festivals to electronic literature collections. Film festivals (and television networks) can showcase the heirs to Flash animation. Even as ActionScript increasingly was incorporated as the major driving force for the platform, the traditional timeline animation tools remained primary in the interface and were only removed in the programmer-focused Flex and Flash Builder.

ActionScript could also enable animation built from outside the timeline, but it ultimately produced results that resembled traditional animation, as the math experiments here demonstrate. However, many Flash works began to take advantage of interactivity, and thus were ideally suited for the home computer experience. These works build on the same libraries and code affordances added to ActionScript to support game development. While early ActionScript interactivity was severely limited and based on a button-pushing model designed for interfaces, the needs of game designers varied wildly (as we addressed earlier). Flash artists take advantage of the whole spectrum of Flash's affordances, while further pushing many of these in unexpected directions in the crafting of new arguments and aesthetic expression. Flash's affordances serve as a playground for the artistic rhetoric of networked spaces while bringing the mechanisms of the avant-garde to digital expressions in new media publics.

Rhetoric through Flash Processes

Flash's role in shaping new media art and rhetoric cannot be considered in isolation: it is one platform of many used for this type of expression. Works in Flash are part of what Noah Wardrip-Fruin defines as expressive processing: the "harnessing" of computational processes for crafting media for "authorial expression" (Wardrip-Fruin 2009, 411). Flash is an ideal platform for authorial expression because of its suitability to the amateur or independent developer. Indeed, in most of the works discussed here, one person was responsible for the entire production—a very different development scenario than the commercial studio approach to developing interactive objects or even animation, as we discussed in chapter 2. The extension of Flash via libraries such as Flixel makes creation of interactive media more accessible to the solo creator, but it also imbues a recognizable common aesthetics among many works of expressive Flash, recalling the definition of "Flashimation" or Manovich's "Generation Flash." Wardrip-Fruin posits that "digital fictions define their own versions of digital media processes in widespread use—or employ versions of these processes defined for use with digital media authoring tools" (43). Chang and Voge repurposed the conventional animation tools of the Flash platform to create an unexpected experience, while also taking some novel affordances offered by Flash 8 to new levels, such as the full-screen browser view and with it the potentially overwhelming nature of a Flash animation constructed boldly to involve sensory overload. Likewise, their choice to reject the traditional media categories of Flash positions their redefinition of Flash's processes. As Pressman notes, Chang and Voge use "Flash as a means of challenging the expectations associated with mainstream electronic literature, Korean art culture, and the end products of specific software"—the processes are essential to the argument (Pressman 2009, 325). The procedures Change and Voge decline to use (including given the user control over the speed of animation, which would radically alter the poetics of the reading experience) are as important as the ones they employ.

These works use Flash as part of making an argument or advancing an artistic statement, generally through what Ian Bogost has termed procedural rhetoric: "the practice of authoring arguments through processes . . . its arguments are made not through the construction of words or images, but through the authorship of rules of behavior, the construction of dynamic models" (Bogost 2007, 28–29). Flash is often a platform of choice for short, easily playable games and interactive art works with serious content. In a dialogue on serious games, games intended to persuade or educate, Kevin Kee pointed to the newsgame *September 12th* by Gonzola Frasca, which allows players to act as the U.S. government by firing on terrorists in a Middle Eastern village (Rockwell and Kee 2011). As Geoffrey M. Rockwell points out, this game could be dismissed as a "5-minute experience with Flash," but it is effective primarily because it is manipulated or played through actions already familiar to Flash game players. It subverts those familiar processes into the tools of its own rhetoric: the player believes he or she can win through following traditional game actions, and destroying the terrorists, but the player ultimately learns there is no way to win (Frasca 2003). The simplicity of the game is its path to greater meaning. As Alec Charles describes, the game features "a philosophical and political argument which it does not articulate so much as it allows the player to explore and perform" (Charles 2009). The simple mechanisms of play are self-defeating, and the player's sense of futility grows with every attempt at action. Newsgames are playable editorials, often with a strong point of view and a clear pressing concern pointing to them. Game-O-Matic, mentioned in chapter 3, is a prime example of Flash's reach and capabilities in this genre. Thus Flash is ideally suited to these works, as Bogost explains: "Flash abstracts the more complex aspects of real-time computer graphics, sound, and input, shortening the development time for newsgames"—while further being "cross-platform by default" (Bogost, Ferrari, and Schweizer 2010). These affordances are particularly valuable because newsgames require immediacy. Flash news games take advantage of the same accessibility to an unsuspecting or non-traditional audience thanks to their juxtaposition with traditional casual Flash game space.

Like the editorial game designers behind newsgames, artists using Flash for the creation of expressive works can experiment with the form in several ways. The most obvious is through the content itself, on which the platform inherently places no limitations, and thus the artist can freely manipulate within the range of his or her own procedural literacy. However, experimental work can further exploit the affordances of the platform itself, extending or reworking elements of thosee underlying boundaries to create something unexpected. Several works also build on the expectations that players or users bring to works created with Flash, breaking those expectations or using the structures of a familiar genre or mechanic to draw attention to a new concept or present a different perspective. This type of experimental work is of the greatest interest to us in understanding the platform, because it probes the abstract entity that is Flash itself, illuminating some of its construction by the act of deconstruction or boundary-crossing.

However, it is difficult to immediately categorize a body of new media art within the Flash landscape. Examining "art" created in Flash is challenging because it first involves proscribing intention to the author, which is often not clearly communicated when a work is one of many within a community such as Newgrounds. Many of these examples are recognizable because of the context in which they were released, such as the gallery showing of Chang and Voge's work. The Flash community itself didn't necessarily offer a context for such work, as Donna Leishman noted in her study: "the contextual or intellectual basis of the FC [Flash community] is incredibly hard to evidence between the lack of published critical discussions and is perhaps part evidenced by Golan Levin's statement: 'I don't really give much consideration to categories like "art", "design", "performance", "science"'" (Leishman 2012). But within some Flash spaces, such as the previously discussed hub Newgrounds, the categorization held some weight. Works identified for their merit have been recognized in the community: 2001 saw the publication of the first *Masters of Flash* books from Friends of ED publishing, and the first Flashforward conference was held in 1999. The conference incorporated a Flash Film Festival, and by the 2004 conference fifteen thousand people attended with festival awards given for interactivity, art, story, and "experimental" works (FlashForward 2004).

Given this focus on intention and placement (and avoiding the larger argument of whether games are art, which at this point has been exhausted by the game studies community, and more broadly the problem of how digital works are categorized within the larger traditions of galleries and artistic gatekeeping), we will also be considering examples of interactive art that reveal a clear expressive intention and illuminate the role of the platform in defining the types of interactions such art relies upon. Among those, metagames, or games that use the structure of games to comment on the nature of gaming, and serious games, or games with an educational or persuasive intention as their primary modus, are most common on Flash. Flash's suitability for widely distributed short-form games makes it ideal for immediate commentary or expressing a quick thought. Within these experiments the accessibility of Flash is also crucial: to refer to chapter 4, the suitability of Flash as a programming environment for non-programmer is valuable for solo artists looking to build interactive expressions without a strong technical background. Additional libraries, such as Flixel, have further made particular types of expression more accessible and thus more common rhetorical tools for those exploring the capabilities of interactivity as expressive medium within Flash's ecosystem. We'll compare a few examples of art games made with Flixel as examples of how libraries of this kind both regulate and promote expression by providing a limited palette within the Flash platform.

Defining New Media Art

There are many ways to potentially define and recognize artistry as created through the Flash platform and to examine how Flash enables the creation of interactive art. Certainly, there is the artistry tied to production methods and considerations inherent in any Flash work, as Hillman Curtis describes in his introduction to a 2002 book examining the best of then state-of-the-art Flash design: "It wasn't long before I learned, as the title designers I admired surely had, the value of restraint. In fact, it was through struggling to find ways to design motion graphics that could work without download bars that I learned about repetition, pacing, and economy. Experimenting with Flash and making mistakes taught me, more than anything had before, how to focus my work and shed any element that isn't absolutely necessary" (Curtis 2002).

Flash's continual state of evolution as a platform constantly offered new opportunities to any designer—each update extended the affordances further. However, the fundamental genres of work that the Flash platform supported were refined through the process Curtis describes, and with that refinement came growing recognition of Flash's potential for art. In animation, this had already developed through the mainstreaming of Flash animation through traditional gatekeepers. But Flash's affordances now made it relatively easy to deviate from established genres, and in doing so fully explore the nature of Flash as a platform for interactive art.

The examples gathered here can be found under many genres, as the Flash platform now permitted a diversity of expression that is hard to categorize. Writing in 2009, Wardrip-Fruin commented that Flash in particular offered a platform for "interactive animations," or fusions between the two genres of Flash production we've noted previously for their dominance of Flash creative expression. The term "interactive animation" recalls the term "interactive cinema," which Kevin Veale (2112) describes as "an experientially distinctive form of storytelling that is not adequately described by either videogame or cinematic engagement in isolation. They are texts of nuance through responsibility, and yet they are uncomplicated to the point where there are no/few skills to be practiced, as would occur in a more ludic and gamelike framework: they are powerful because of what is experienced, and how it is experienced, rather than the skill required to overcome the challenges involved in the journey." The properties Veale notes could also be ascribed to the Flash platform, which offered ludic frameworks on top of a cinematic or animated primary metaphor. This hybridity is a fundamental duality in the affordances of the Flash platform, as opposed to the fusion of toolsets required to achieve the same types of interactivity in film. The increasing power (and speed) of ActionScript did not eliminate the timeline, and the metaphors of traditional animation and keyframes were thus never abandoned among Flash's chief affordances. The link to animation present inherently in the Flash platform (and exploited in many of the works we'll examine in this chapter) reflects the layering of new media work that Manovich noted: "the visual culture of a computer age is cinematographic in its appearance, digital on the level of its material, and computational (i.e., software driven) in its logic" (Manovich 2001, 161). Flash post-2004 embodied this layering in the very architecture of the platform, particularly as the accessibility and strength of the computational (ActionScript) layer grew, encouraging the type of expressive new media works we'll examine throughout this chapter.

Flash Poetics

When defining interactive cinema, Veale notes one Flash work in particular that demonstrates the power of this type of new media art experience: Daniel Benmergui's 2008 *I wish I were the Moon*. In *I wish I were the Moon*, the player controls a camera taking Polaroid-esque snapshots of the game's characters: a boy sitting on a moon and a girl in a boat, with a bird flying by and shooting stars in the sky. The unrequited love at the start of the story is clear: the girl is in love with the distant boy, and the boy is in love with the moon, staring up at its inaccessibility even as she gazes longingly at him (Benmergui 2008).

The player can reach several different endings by rearranging the objects in the scene. Placing the girl on the moon ends with separation and the phrase "I am your moon," while placing both the boy and girl atop the moon results in a happy union even as the moon sinks, revealing the ominous phrase "If I can't have you . . ." at the top of the screen. Aesthetically, the pixel artistry of *I wish I were the Moon* (as shown in figure 5.1) is very different from the typical Flash aesthetic. It defies the vector art illustration model incorporated in Flash to create the feeling of low-resolution graphics common to early 8-bit console platforms. Bogost notes the work and "the expressive six-pixel eyes" as among those demonstrating that "no matter the level of abstraction, proceduralist works don't equate higher abstraction with lower production value. Where image, sound, and text is present, it's carefully selected and incorporated into the system that forms the rest of the game" (Bogost 2011b, 15). Benmergui explained the work's inspiration as textually grounded, with no initial concept of game mechanics:

> It was actually a combination of two things [that] inspired me to make the game. One was from Italo Calvino's short story "The Distance of the Moon," which left me feeling like I had a knot in my stomach after I had reached the ending. Then one day while I was listening to Enigma's "Sitting on the Moon," and I was struck with an image in my head. The game as it is now looks exactly like that image I had thought of at that moment. I had no idea where I was going gameplay-wise, although the camera mechanic was something I already had from an old prototype. (Tim W. 2008)

The work is clearly game-inspired in its appearance, but procedurally far removed from gameplay. The manipulation of the objects evokes Flash's own metaphor of movieclips as movable objects, suggesting that

Figure 5.1
I wish I were the Moon, 2008, Daniel Benmergui

the player "authors" each ending through simple actions not unlike working in the Flash GUI. The penultimate function in the program reveals the simplicity enabled by the object representation, even as it illuminates the combinations and conditions of interactivity and their sometimes sorrowful endings. Even without knowledge of code or procedures, the logical tests are immediately apparent:

```
public function ending():String
{
if(boat.y > water.y)
```

```
{
return "Sunk boat Secret Ending";
}
else
if(fireworks)
{
return "Such a pretty sky";
}
else
if(countFlowers() > 0)
{
return "Do not forget me";
}
else
if(boy.isGone() && girl.isGone() && water.isSubmerged(moon))
{
return "If I can't have you...";
}
else
if((boy.drown || girl.drown) && !water.isSubmerged(moon))
{
return "Tragedy";
}
else
if(boy.hasMoon && !girl.drown)
{
return "Bring me the Moon";
}
else
if(gull.goneBoy)
{
return "No reason to live";
}
else
if((!boy.isFalling) && girl.isOnBoat() && moon.isGone())
{
return "Lost Love";
}
else
if(boy.isOnBoat() && girl.isOnMoon() && girl.isHarping())
{
return "I am your Moon";
}
else
if(!boy.isGone() && gull.goneGirl)
{
return "Be Free";
}
return null;
}
```

This sequence of code illuminates the simplicity of states of happiness or despair: each potential love story is reduced to its essential binary components. Much of this code is familiar to the standard tenets of scripting, but it is telling how this sequence of ActionScript is a story in itself: the properties attached to each character reveal the narrative. This simplicity is particularly powerful given the unpredictability and lack of transparency of the game's mechanics to the player. Line Hollis refers to this as the "gulf of execution" at work, since "it is not only unclear what your actions will do, but also which of your movements may be considered actions" (Hollis 2009). The code is readable by humans, but the player will never get to read it: the system of Flash compiles the code and its revealing details so that the patterns of the game are just out of the player's reach. This same code could not appear in a JavaScript game, where the player could simply view the source to reveal its secrets, without giving away the mystery and ruining the allure of the secret ending.

Benmergui's code revolves around each element being aware of its status. For example, all of the expressions in the game are procedurally generated based on the current state of the character. A character could be in a state of seeking, where the eyes are drawn so as to follow the object desired. This small procedural detail, implemented through a simple switch statement and some graphic drawing commands, cements the animus of the characters and positions the audience as responsible for their fate even as it penalizes the player's good intentions—as when the player places the couple on the moon, only to create the ultimate tragedy. The current location of an object relative to others determines its trajectory or animation, whether it be toward the ocean or riding off the screen on a gull. Benmergui's code takes full advantage of both the DisplayList and Flash's more advanced functions. Two in particular are essential to the game's aesthetic: one is the ability for Flash to record its own display pixels, used in the action of taking a photograph. Another is Flash's ability to "introspect" or be able to programmatically find objects by their class, which is used extensively for counting objects. As Benmergui mentioned, he reused an existing piece of code for taking pictures and fashioned it into a new piece.

The narrative elements of Benmergui's work draw heavily on both literature and games. This type of experience design falls under the categorization of electronic literature as defined by the Electronic Literature Organization (in a committee led by Joe Tabbi in 2006): "work with an important literary aspect that takes advantage of the capabilities and contexts provided by the stand-alone or the networked computer" (Hayles 2007). Flash's close ties to animation make it a strong platform for such narrative works, although it is far from the only platform used by electronic literature (hypertext, etc.) It's worth noting that the definition of electronic literature is already very platform-intrinsic, if agnostic to the particular computing hardware. Leonardo Flores's series on electronic literature, *I Love E-Poetry*, lists Flash as a technology alongside the animated gif, Basic, Director, DHTML, HTML, HyperCard, JavaScript, Perl, processing, Python, Ruby and Twitter. Of these technologies and platforms, Flash is one of the more accessible while still offering a range of expressive processing possibility when compared to the affordances of more limited forms such as HTML and HyperCard. The first volume of the *Electronic Literature Collection* includes several diverse Flash pieces, including Flash as a keyword with the description "a commercial system particularly useful for vector-based animation" and twenty-six listed works in a collection of only sixty produced between 1994 and 2006 (Hayles et al. 2006). This disproportionate representation shows the platform's strong appeal to visual and narrative artists who used Flash to create kinetic works as well as gamelike works.

There are several examples of electronic literature works that take advantage of the affordances of Flash. One of the most prominent Flash artists within the community is Jason Nelson, who uses Flash to develop a poetics of motion. Scott Rettberg describes the feeling of layered meaning juxtaposed with digital layers in Nelson's work, as Nelson requires readers "to reject the web convention of a two-dimensional screen and insist that we navigate deeper, swimming into a three-dimensional axis. We navigate in layers between objects, such as a dumpster and a credit card, or a hamburger and a gun, or a bottle of prescription pills and a wedding cake, or a sofa and a communications tower. Along the way, we might encounter poetic meditations" (Rettberg 2010). This use of Flash is dictated both by the platform and by Nelson's own artistic sensibility, as he described in an interview: "I still really love Flash as an artistic/game creating tool. Nearly all of my artworks involve layering of odd poetic content, of coaxing sounds into icons into moving drawings into text triggered by a lurching character. And Flash makes that easy and visually compelling to create" (Stuart 2011). Works such as Nelson's *Game, Game, Game and Again Game* use platformer controls such as moving with the arrow keys and jumping combined with unexpected animation, flashing text, hand-drawn art, and layered experiences to probe at the nature of consumer aesthetics (Nelson 2007). The hybridity of Nelson's experiments rejects any simple duality of interactive art versus game, while demonstrating the potential of play in giving the reader-player agency in driving the experience and the revealing of expression.

Nelson's realization of Flash aesthetics demonstrates the layering of content and the transformation from the affordances of one medium to the next as a fundamental and desirable property of his works' interface. This recalls Manovich's point about digital tools: "One general effect of the digital revolution is that avant-garde aesthetic strategies [such as collage, painting of film, etc.] came to be embedded in the commands and interface metaphors of computer software. In short, the avant-garde became materialized in a computer" (2001, 300). Nelson describes many of his works as art games, a category that some Flash communities have even embraced, and his work clearly embodies the avant-garde aesthetics turned platform affordances as fundamental tools of his expressive palette. His early works are part of the "second-generation" of electronic literature that Hayles noted as emerging in 2002 as part of a transformation to the "fully multimedia" moving "deeper into the machine" (Hayles 2002). The Flash platform was a driving force in enabling this movement, particularly in the hybridity of media experiences as fully integrated rather than isolated in a hypertextual collage. But the journey of electronic literature into the machine was only beginning, as new works would continue to investigate not just what the Flash platform made accessible but what it could be made to create through code.

Creative Code

The exploration of computational logic behind the "cinematographic" appearance of Flash works as Manovich described can be seen in several different ways, but it is easily recognizable in play with computer graphics. Such experiments produce results that are not inherently interactive, but still distinct from the planned animations of the traditional timeline. The book *Flash Math Creativity* documented these types of experiments in pre-MX Flash in 2001, although the entire book was revised for the new affordances of ActionScript 2.0 and Flash MX in 2004. One of the profiled artists, Glen Rhodes, expressed his interest in the mathematical creation of imagery: "As the experiments went on . . . the beauty left the real world, and entered the just-as-beautiful digital, numeric, mathematical realm" (Peters et al. 2004, 19). Rhodes credits Flash with being a space to take all his experiences and "combine them," drawing from music, mathematics, and games (19). In these experiments, the timeline holds a simple graphical element for the algorithm to manipulate, thus still drawing on the original affordances of Flash allied with computational expression:

```
For (var i:Number=0; i<120; i++) {
var nm: MovieClip = attachMovie("petal," "petal" + I, i);
nm._x = Stage.width /2;
nm._y = Stage.height / 2;
nm._rotation = Math.random() *360;
```

```
nm._xscale = nm._yscale—Math.random() * 100 +20;
}
```

The original algorithm forms a rose: varying it slightly by eliminating the random rotation and instead using fixed scale and rotation in increments creates seashells, fireworks, and alien objects. Here, the MovieClip and Stage objects that timeline animation relies upon are fused with the increasing procedural capabilities of ActionScript to create art that is primarily interactive through iterating its code, not unlike the line of Commodore 64 BASIC examined in *10 PRINT* (Montfort et al. 2012). That line of code is most notable for its seemingly endless mutability, and thus its encouragement of computational play and experimentation. Likewise, the forward to *Flash Math Creativity* encourages this attitude: "Creation's not all it's about. Once you've fashioned your masterpiece, you have to change it . . . in Flash this is the easiest thing in the world to do. Change one variable and you change the whole piece, sometimes subtly, and sometimes astronomically . . . just grab the files from the site, open them in Flash, and do your best to break them" (Peters et al. 2004). This is a communal model for interactivity not unlike the sharing of code and resources described in chapter 4. The artistic expression is realized not through a finished piece, but through the potential in the algorithms themselves, unlocked only through further creative exploitation.

This model of creativity through breaking code doesn't stop at other creator's works; it extends to breaking and extending the platform itself. In the introduction to *Flash 3D: Animation, Interactivity, and Games*, the authors write: "The first thing you should know about 3D and Flash is that there is no 3D in Flash," a tongue-in-cheek acknowledgment that their entire work is intended to provide hacks for something not well-supported by Flash's affordances at the time (Hague and Jackson 2006, 1). Instead, the guide suggests ways to build the illusion of 3D without the supporting framework another platform might hold through defining a mathematical transformation to provide the illusion of a z-axis where none exists. Experiments with 3D in Flash art predate any real support by the platform, as 3D transformation for objects on the Display List wasn't introduced into Flash Player until version 10 in October 2008, with Stage 3D graphics acceleration introduced in version 11 in October 2011. Just as the creator of the first Flash pinball game hacked together a solution, so too would creators who wanted to introduce 3D—the Friends of ED published a collection of *Flash 3D Creativity* in 2003, before Flash MX 2004 introduced object-oriented programming and well before Adobe Flash CS4 introduced 3D object manipulation in 2008.

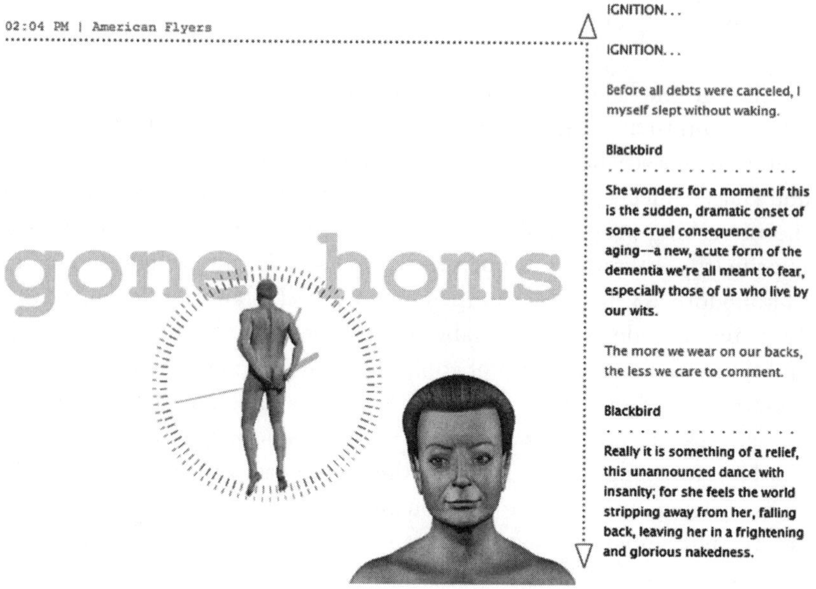

IGNITION. . .

IGNITION. . .

Before all debts were canceled, I myself slept without waking.

Blackbird

. . . .

She wonders for a moment if this is the sudden, dramatic onset of some cruel consequence of aging—a new, acute form of the dementia we're all meant to fear, especially those of us who live by our wits.

The more we wear on our backs, the less we care to comment.

Blackbird

. . . .

Really it is something of a relief, this unannounced dance with insanity; for she feels the world stripping away from her, falling back, leaving her in a frightening and glorious nakedness.

Figure 5.2
Pax, 2003, Stuart Moulthrop

One example of this incorporation of the illusion of 3D motion came from the electronic literature community. Stuart Moulthrop released *Pax* in 2003: a time-driven exploration of human experience with falling 3D bodies, as shown in figure 5.2, with movement through space, narrative, and thought coexisting. Moulthrop described his intention to build *Pax* as a "textual instrument" combining prerendered 3D graphics with text delivered through Flash as propelled by the reader's focus and exploration of the falling bodies (Moulthrop 2008). Moulthrop describes the navigation of the work:

The reader/player elicits and assembles text by interacting with characters who drift through the main section of the screen. These floating figures cycle through animations that make them seem to spin through the air . . . moving over the outline of a character arrests that character's progress and fixes the character within a superimposed clock face. Clicking at this point causes the system to retrieve a passage of text and add it to a scrolling field on the right-hand side of the screen. The text comes in two flavors or types: a generalized, algorithmically generated near-nonsense that represents the random babble of the unconscious; or a more coherent prose passage that represents some focused comment on the character's predicament. (Moulthrop 2013)

The algorithmic coexists with the intentional, structured experience:

```
//PERSONAE lists name stems of all character movies
_root.personae = new Array("f1,"""f4,"""f6,"""f8,"""f9,"""f11,"""f12,"
"m5,"""m6,"""m7,"""m8,"""m10,"""m11,"""m12");
```

(code from Stuart Moulthrop, *Pax*, 2003)

Moulthrop's code makes extensive use of timers and arrays to assemble an intricate machine that acts akin to a Mad Libs generator. He coordinates "story time" with the progression of real time, using randomness to select between sentiments and possible insertions in a piece of text. Each of these segments is encoded as part of an Array in the source code. In this piece of code, Moulthrop initializes each character with a movie, giving the name to the variable "Personae" and evoking in a way that no member of the audience will witness the metaphor of the stage that is always on Flash developers' minds. In this case, MovieClips contain individual character animation and sentiments, and the choice of variable name is more in line with expectations compared to the more awkward constructions of hitRecord and prevRandChar. The code itself fluctuates between the poetic and the algorithmic: though it is systemically an unreadable part of the work, and not necessarily easy for a human to read even once the code is revealed, it shapes the DNA for each "Personae."

The work itself emerges from this DNA, its patterns changing with each iteration and the user's choices. Moulthrop noted himself that *Pax* is meant for "momentary consumption": the ability to export the text of a session was deliberately eliminated, despite the fact that it would have been relatively simple to encode such functionality in Flash (Moulthrop 2008). A published excerpt highlights the poetic excerpts and their focus on fleeting thoughts:

What do you do about the blood?
Our concerns include: peace, annoyance, zero sum, suicide, war speak, suspect.
Di Laffing

. . . .

Fear no evil.
Can you conceive of fear without junk mail?
Di Laffing

. . . .

So maybe I am dead, and so are all those other confused-looking folks who by the way don't seem to have read the memo about casual dress in the afterlife. Did someone do this to us? Do I care?
After this, all they taught us comes to be radiant with hope.

mira

The procedural combined with the deliberate and coherent leads to meaning through juxtaposition. While the code itself cannot reveal the literary text, the generated work appears to have authorial intention behind each element even when it reaches what Moulthrop called "random babble": even the random is encoded.

In *Pax* we can see piecemeal the affordances of Flash in 2003 combined to produce an unusual interface for "reading" and the ability of ActionScript to enable procedural generation alongside an interactive animation, building prerendered 3D art into a 2D engine. Here, electronic literature presses on the framework of its constraining platform, and in doing so demonstrates some of the capabilities that would eventually be more completely integrated into the engine: art predicts the platform's future. The construction of code that is highly complex in Moulthrop's work will be rendered simpler by future generations of Flash, but the patterns of the interactions are already present. *Pax* contains a blueprint not only for Flash as coauthor of the work—or co-interpreter, at least, of a procedural DNA—but for the increasing interest in dimensionality of all kinds in Flash works.

The lure of 3D graphics for Flash artists, both amateur and professional, was so great that a number of libraries were developed to implement, in software, the same procedures that 3D engines rely on. These engines handled the projection of a 3D model onto a flat image surface. The most prominent engine was Papervision3D, an open source project developed to allow Flash creators to represent cubes, complex 3D models, and transitions on a website.

The use of Flash for pioneering generative text continues in *Prom Week*, a game where a more sophisticated system determines which text chunks to play based on a simulation of social state. In it, the text used to represent the success or failure of a character's attitudes toward one another is rendered as a short animated conversation drawn largely from templates and filled in with details about the character's gender and status. These database-based approaches to electronic literature represent an edge case in Flash's capabilities, as the platform has no native support of its own for working with text beyond simple strings and concatenations. Moulthrop described this trajectory as follows: the desire to be the *"writing of writers"* systems and to distribute them widely outweighs the challenges of adapting Flash to this end (Moulthrop 2013).

Art Games

Works such as the experiments of Nelson and Moulthrop's can also be placed alongside or within the category of "art games." This is a categorization that Newgrounds recognizes in a collection that again privileges the intention behind the game and seeks to group the works under a shared definition: "Some games are made and exhibited as art. The intent isn't necessarily to provide the player with a challenge or addictive mechanic, but rather to convey a message, elicit an emotion or create a memorable experience" (Newgrounds n.d.). While the collection helps distinguish these games from other works in the community, there is no clear place in the category hierarchy for them: most of the games are found under "Action—Platformer—Other" thanks to a common reliance on platformer controls. As of July 2013, there are fewer than one hundred games in the category, ranging from Benmergui's work to visual novels and a "short story platformer." These art games demonstrate the evolution of Flash aesthetics and rhetoric.

One name spotted often within the art games category is SilverStitch, creator of the *Colour My Heart* Flash game and its sequels. The games are simple platformers set in a sketched black-and-white world. The games (particularly the first) are short and easy to "beat" with their basic platformer mechanics, but exploring the world and fulfilling the quest for emotional fulfillment is more difficult. SilverStitch's description of his own process in learning and building Flash art games recalls the iterative nature of the Flash math experiments: "My original physics 'engine' for the first Colour game was based off an old flash physics engine I found, but I didn't like it too much so I re-wrote it. Over time though, with every new project I worked on, I fixed it up and tweaked it. The best you can do is keep working at coding and animating over and over again, over-coming obstacles as they come and trying to better yourself" (SilverStitch 2013).

Other games directly exploit the rhetoric of their genres. For instance, *You Only Live Once* offers a classic *Mario* opening where a man's girlfriend is kidnapped and he goes on a quest to save her. Once the player dies and reaches the "Game Over" screen, he is presented with a familiar option, "Continue?" However, pressing continue yields not another chance but a vision of his girlfriend finding the body and calling for an ambulance to the stage, and another "Game Over" screen. A series of progressive "Continue?" animations shows the consequences of death: news reports reminding fellow would-be rescuers to contact the police rather than engaging in vigilante justice, the arrest of the boss for not making platforms accessible to disabled persons, and finally a memorial site. The game moves from apparently interactive play to passive, cinematic experience, evoking both sides of the platform's original dichotomy of coding. John Tynes argues for defining these metagames as "engagist," works that reject the somewhat derogatory label of "escapist" and instead provide "tools and opportunities for participants to explore and experiment in [a] setting in ways that real life prohibits or discourages" (Tynes 2008). Flash games, by nature of their accessibility and ubiquity, created the genre of escapist casual games. Metagames flip those elements to draw attention to the engagement/escapist dichotomy.

Likewise, Flash metagames such as *Achievement Unlocked* choose one mechanism familiar from the genre and take them to an extreme (Armor Games 2008). The game space is a very straightforward platformer, with most blocks buildable with the Flash internal graphics interface and a playable elephant sprite, all in the single-color vector aesthetic associated with Flash. The loading screen includes the message "Don't worry, metagaming is all that matters," and the side of the game screen includes ninety-nine achievements for everything from staying alive for ten seconds to "Too Much Free Time." This focus on achievements mocks the interest in achievement incorporation throughout the rest of the Newgrounds community (and games at large). Around this same time, achievement systems were being integrated into Flash communities. Kongregate integrated badges that incorporate across games, and new start-up HeyZap launch a virtual currency based on achievements in its Flash game portal (Kincaid 2009). In 2008, a forum discussion on Newgrounds addressed the idea of adding achievements community-wide, with less than enthusiastic responses: "So much for Everything by Everyone then" and "Everything by Everyone; we must stick to that, and avoid separating 'noob' and 'pro' simply by somebody's profile" (Newgrounds 2008). Here, the metagame becomes an editorial on the possible future of Flash gaming and the desirability of the achievement system, not just the ease of implementation.

Other Flash art games draw attention to the very experience of play and to a fundamental contradiction inherent in a platform that is simultaneously highly dependent on networks yet usually solo. Eli Piilonen's *The Company of Myself* is a Flash art game (released to Newgrounds) where the player is a hermit who "assists" himself through shadow selves through

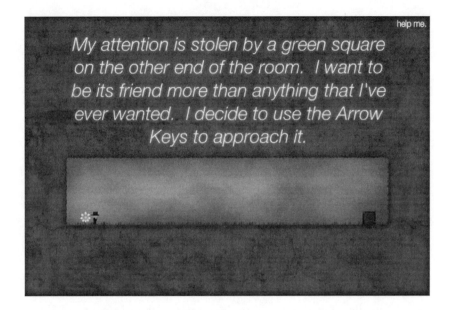

My attention is stolen by a green square on the other end of the room. I want to be its friend more than anything that I've ever wanted. I decide to use the Arrow Keys to approach it.

help me.

Figure 5.3
The Company of Myself, 2009, Eli Piilonen

a platformer/puzzle game. The game begins with a textual monologue: "The first thing you need to understand is that I am alone. I've been alone for a pretty long time now. I'm used to it. I'm content. . . . I generally face the same day-to-day problems as every other person, except that when every other person gets stuck, they have their friends and associates to back them up. I don't . . . I used to find joy in the company of others. Now, I only have the company of myself" (Piilonen, Marcetic, and Carney 2009).

The internal text, as shown in figure 5.3, equates the platformer mechanics to the experience of solitude. "I search for reasons why I don't desire companionship. I settle on avoidance of the issue. I can clearly get by without others, anyways" appears on the screen accompanied by a puzzle where the character can only proceed by carrying himself across a chasm using his shadow selves. The player eventually encounters the character's former companion, Kathryn, and for a while can jointly solve puzzles through cooperating with her. "I never expected the end to come so quickly" appears on the screen as the player reaches a puzzle where the only way to succeed is to allow Kathryn to fall into a chasm. As the player exits the final level, the following message is displayed: "Are you really leaving?" This echoes the "more complex solo play" Tom Tyler notes as distinct to digital gameplay (Tyler 2008).

Flash as Palette

Many of the works examined here rely on platformer mechanics and controls for their interactivity, which is not surprising thanks to Flash's accommodation of this type of interface. Additional libraries make using these mechanics even more accessible. As we discussed at the end of chapter 4, Flixel is one of the most popular of these libraries. Flixel provides a framework for many of the primary elements of a platformer, and that framework can be seen etched into the design elements and play patterns of works created with its resources. In part because of its simplification of the algorithmic and procedural aspects of building a game, Flixel is a powerful tool for artists who want to create interactive works. The library provides a blueprint that can be extended. The MIT Game Lab used the library to create the browser-based game *Elude*, a game designated as a "serious" game with the intention of revealing the experience of depression to those who haven't suffered from the condition. As a Flixel game, *Elude* uses the controls of a basic platformer, its mechanics adapted to allow for a plunge into depression and an "ascent to happiness" (Gambit 2010). However, there is one additional control: the spacebar offers the ability to "resonate" by connecting with "passion objects"—birds whose state changes from white-gray to green as the player reaches out. This is not so distant from a standard Flash platformer as the objects are in a sense power ups, as well as triggers toward a positive endgame state but with a different expressive resonance. Climbing trees to reach the fresh air at the top becomes a metaphor for finding happiness in the face of escalating obstacles. Lead designer Doris Carmen Rusch noted that "it is easy to lose track of the concept that shall be modeled if one is too concerned too soon with making a game"—a problem libraries like Flixel can eliminate by doing much of the work of "making" (Rusch 2010, 3).

Another Flixel powered art game, Jake Elliott's 2010 *I Can Hold My Breath Forever*, uses elements of the Flash aesthetic and color palette with a pixel art style. The player moves through a very simple platformer with much of the area underwater, pushed on by a timer counting down the ten seconds available between reemerging. Throughout, the player finds letters from a childhood friend. The letters grow increasingly distant, speaking of years spent lost in the cave: "When we were children, I dove into a small pond. Now we are both very old, and it is time for me to stop exploring. I will wait for you here in the water. But there's no need for you to hurry; I can hold my breath forever" (Elliott 2010). The player then finds the lost childhood friend, an octopus. The ending is ambiguous, because the player clearly cannot survive in this deep underwater domain, but examining the code reveals that this ending has been built into a function for victory:

```
if(player.won_game) {
oxygen_timer_display.alpha = 0;
darkness.alpha = 0;
var speed:uint = 400;
var target:FlxPoint = new FlxPoint(world.octopus.x - 16,world.
octopus.y + 4);
```

Here, the choice of the built-in function for "player.won_game" as a designation for this ending condition might change our reading of the game's outcome—at least, when the code is available and not masked by compilation. Of course, this might be a case where the defaults of the Flixel library impose a positive tone on a deliberately ambiguous experience. The code also connects the events to the timer mechanic, an essential part of the game experience: the timer drives the player from oxygen bubble to oxygen bubble in search of the lost friend. Elliott described his intention to play with time as experienced by the self and other: "That's a really weird experience, like you're talking about getting a letter from somebody, and they're on this other path. And it seems like it's been a long time, but it also seems like it hasn't really been that long, but things have diverged so much, it's like, really striking. That estrangement is a really strange feeling" (Frank 2012). The game's mechanics encourage the player to literally dive deeper and deeper, but the concrete meaning is elusive thanks to the restructuring of the platformer's roles and systems.

Flash has served as a platform for expressive processing, from interactive art to art game and all the overlapping spaces in between. These works simultaneously demonstrate how the expected limits of the platform can be overcome and how those same limits have informed an artistic rhetoric. Most prominently, the common reliance on platformer controls moving through a 2D space reveals how the most accessible features of Flash become a fundamental part of the artistic palette—an evolution further reinforced by the development of libraries (including Flixel) that make building certain interactions easier. It is no coincidence that the same patterns found in beginner controllers and quick start libraries are embedded in most of the examples here, along with many other art and metagames. N. Katherine Hayles suggested that Flash was one platform behind the move "deeper into the machine," an apt description for the role of the platform in transforming the web from a surface experience to a more interactive space (Hayles 2002). Likewise, the increasing attention of the Flash platform stewards to the needs of power users (as reflected in

the sophistication of ActionScript 3.0) emphasizes the increasing importance placed on procedural complexity for the platform, even as the ease
of creation is threatened. These interactive experiences that don't fall into
the typology of game, animation, or advertisement are not as evocative as
"Flash games" of an expected experience, but instead illustrate what the
platform's fusion of animation, web context, and game affordances could
lend itself to creating.

Free and Open?

The War for Control

The ubiquity of Flash depended as much on its perception as its technical capabilities. When it worked, it was virtually invisible, showcasing instead the content. But when it became a point of contention between Android and iPhone, between closed technologies and modern, open standards, Flash became an ideological warzone. The terms "free" and "open" in software contexts refer to a stance on subtle variations of power. They (and their opposites) designate control and ownership: control over the expression of an intellectual property, and ownership of rights pertaining to it, including reproduction and modification. These properties have inspired the Free Software and Open Source movements, both of which agree that software licenses should protect "user's essential freedoms." In the definition set forth by the Free Software Foundation, these include "the freedom to run, copy, distribute, study, change and improve the software" (Free Software Foundation 2013). The Open Source Initiative (OSI) provides a broader set of licenses and differing guidelines on what software conforms to its definition. While Flash is fundamentally a proprietary platform (being owned by various corporations), the perception of Flash has been shaped by many contributions and extensions to its ecosystem outside of Adobe's control. Those contributions, which include editors, players, and software, make Flash more than the sum of the development system and player. From the beginning, the Flash ecosystem provided an open API and built on existing standards, such as ECMAScript, Flex, the

Tamarin Virtual Machine, and others. These adoptions were as much practical necessity as ideological stratagem, as inventing a new language standard or concealing the inner workings of the code was counterproductive at best.

Even with the pragmatic necessity, Adobe needed rhetorical strength and ideological high ground to win over developers' hearts and minds. The pervasiveness of the platform required complicity among its developers and partners to maintain its status. It was thus at odds with the reality that it has only partial control over the context of the Flash platform. Most problematically for its user-developer base, the choices Adobe makes are ultimately motivated by business reasons, and not ideological mandates. Flash Player depends heavily on its host environment for its value; as soon as any company refuses to host the virtual machine in its operating system or browser, the content can suddenly be rendered unusable. This type of conflict did come to pass with Apple and the rise of mobile devices, as we will examine in chapter 7, with immediate consequences. Flash's openness is as much a defense from this type of imposed obscurity as it is Adobe's position on whether platforms must be open to be successful. Cooperation on all levels of the ecosystem is essential to sustaining a platform that strives to be universal. Unlike a console, a software platform cannot control many layers of its underlying infrastructure. Flash has no dedicated environment. It requires access on its host systems to act as it pleases, and it can be rejected. That tenuous existence is a defining trait of the Flash ecosystem, and it cannot be overlooked when considering how the platform's choices have shaped the web—and vice versa.

A software platform exists in a much more abstracted space than hardware platforms do, but like hardware platforms, it is impossible to separate the high-level business strategy and context from the low-level affordances that defines a platform. In this chapter, we'll be looking at how Flash's features and evolution took place in a context of conflicting forces influencing the degree to which Adobe opened the platform and negotiated control with its developers and the hardware platforms it resided on. After all, Flash cannot be run without several other platforms coexisting: it might run within Flash Player, embedded within Internet Explorer, or on a PC manufactured by Dell running Microsoft Windows 7. That list represents some of the competing corporate interests. Flash's owners made several choices regarding control, particularly in light of its uneasy position as a piggybacker on browsers and operating systems. Very few platforms have tried to spread so wildly, riding on top of whatever software and hardware is available, without ending up committed to one ecosystem. Adobe's expansion of the reach of Flash included targeting enterprise applications with the introduction of Flex. Adobe also explored the mobile space initially with feature phones and Flash Lite, and eventually with Adobe Integrated Runtime's cross compilation using what is known as a low-level virtual machine (LLVM). "Cross compilation" is where the byte code of the original virtual machine is translated directly into another hardware platform's machine code using a virtual machine to translate the machine code at a low level. Being able to compile to another platform extends the reach of the platform and correspondingly increases the number of interested developers. The vitality of a software platform ebbs and flows with the engagement of its developers. This engagement is directly tied to both the number of developers actively developing content on the platform and the number of users they can reach.

For a software developer on any platform, the platform represents an investment. If a platform's future comes into question, the loss of momentum alone can cause developers to question their commitment to authoring for it. In open source platforms, the risks are at least more transparent among the primary users and developers, and each participant accepts the unknown but also has a degree of control. Open platforms can fragment: participants can pull the project in different directions, forking the code, branching off to create new architecture, and often creating competing standards in the process, as is already the case on much of the web. Volunteer projects that operate purely as free, open source software are sometimes perceived as lacking cohesion and predictability and often require technical knowledge to use. In contrast, a corporate steward controls the strategy and roadmap for its proprietary platform, even though many invite contributions and bug reports from their community of developers. A steward's motivations are usually in line with the community, but the ultimate objective is to reap a return on their investment. As we've discussed, this doesn't always align with the platform's developers, and the large shifts in strategy are subject to the realities of the market.

While professional computer scientists often adapt their skillsets to suit the job environment, artists have enjoyed Flash for its relatively uniform and consistent environment for developing multimedia. These users are least likely to upgrade Flash if their needs are ignored: recall the *Homestar Runner* team, described in chapter 2, and the birthday card for the team's favored version of Flash and its artist-friendly system. These artists may not be vocally advancing the opening of the platform's source, but they can certainly be among the first to take advantage of libraries and knowledge made possible by open source projects. While not running the free and open source software (FOSS) movement, many of them benefit from its influence on corporate policy and the availability of alternatives to existing products, such as more affordable Flash authoring programs and more versatile third party libraries that replace or supplant native capabilities. For these users, Flash can potentially be the best of both worlds—proprietary enough to be directed in its evolution and consistent in the presence of the runtime on user's browsers, but open enough to have supplemental development tools and more options for solving challenges along the way.

"Open source" describes a number of conditions related to the licensing of source code in addition to making the source code available along with the program. The growing number and availability of open source projects are seen as a step toward a world where software can be modified, extended, and understood, but in reality the choice to use an open source license has multiple motivations. The terms of that license differ markedly; both "copyleft" licenses that require software that modifies the original also be put under a copyleft license and more "permissive" licenses that can be included in proprietary systems are considered open source. Unlike in the free software world, where programmers come together under a skilled and charismatic software developer, open source projects don't always invite uninhibited modifications, experiments, and redistribution. It is also rhetorically set against proprietary, despite many proprietary software projects using and extending open source projects. In his definitive work *The Cathedral and the Bazaar*, Eric Raymond analyzes the economics and realities of large-scale open source projects and the effects of organizational differences necessitated by open source projects (Raymond 1999). Raymond contrasts two models for software development: the cathedral model, where developers are geniuses working in isolation (the primary method espoused by iconic designers like Steve Jobs), and the bazaar model, where the community of the marketplace brings many buyers and sellers together to play their part in development. In his study of the Commodore Amiga, Jimmy Maher notes that after Amiga's developer Commodore "ceded its expected role as high priest of the Amiga community," an open community could to some extent take over (Maher 2012). By contrast, with Flash Adobe strove perpetually to both maintain the sanctity of the cathedral and provide provisions for a bazaar outside. This arrangement incorporated developer feedback on early builds while maintaining at first complete control over the contents of the official libraries. The reality of the platform resembled less a cathedral of software architecture and more a city of related products that shared blueprints. The Adobe Integrated Runtime (AIR) project shared aspects of Flash Player, with both relying on libraries. The bazaar aspects of the approach included alternate cathedrals and even competing development tools.

Flash has demonstrated that the development of a software platform can attract and sustain contributions and growth despite not being either a cathedral or a bazaar. Instead it presented a fusion of the two approaches, borrowing ideology and practical benefits from each.

Platforms have historically incorporated open source components, and almost every major software company has had a relationship with opening parts of its platform. Joel West considered the ways in which three companies, IBM, Sun, and Apple, integrated open source software into their strategies in the face of Microsoft's dominant position (West 2003). In his analysis, he revealed that each company employed different ways of incorporating open source to gain an advantage by commoditizing (making a good or service uniformly available) various levels of their value chain. This is similar to Adobe's approach to open source software components, and it recalls any attempt by a corporate producer to reconcile the value of its product with the input, as is described by Lawrence Lessig's hybrid economy. This allows the company to focus resources on the part of the system that provides the most value while relying on users to increase the value of the platform through open efforts.

The value created outside the platform can vary from the tools themselves to the code and runtimes. For instance, IBM commoditized the Eclipse platform by opening it up for others to use, while still maintaining their own premium version. This enabled IBM to receive bug fixes and other benefits of open source software, while still being able to add its proprietary code on top. Adobe also chose Eclipse to be the basis for its programmer-focused development tool, Flex Builder. Flex Builder was the original enterprise development environment for Flex. It was later rebranded as Flash Builder in order to emphasize that the output was a SWF file, and not a separate product altogether, strengthening its connection with the already-established nearly universal platform. Flash Builder was an attempt to address the needs of enterprise users to create standardized applications and hook them up to services such as databases and web APIs. Flash Builder grew to become the primary tool for developing larger Flash applications, including support for the visual arrangement of the Flex library and components.

Adobe Catalyst was an experimental tool that sought to address the growing need for designers to work with Flex components created in Flash Builder. Catalyst was never very widely adopted, but its very presence showed Adobe's effort to court enterprise developers with a product tailored to their needs. Catalyst was an attempt to reconcile the programmatic and inaccessible interface of Flash Builder with the visual feedback provided by the familiar Flash Professional interface. One feature involved switching between states and coordinating animations and the hiding and displaying of elements corresponding to states. A state in a typical application might include a different version of a login screen where the interface showed a registration form instead of a username and password prompt. To replicate a similar screen transition in Flash Professional required moving awkwardly between frames on a timeline. Flash Catalyst provided the capability to export to a clickable HTML version of the application and was intended to ease the prototyping process. The hybrid approach of a designer manipulating an interface that resembled the final output while still using Flex underneath was still awkward, because Flex's syntax and structure was far less accessible to non-coders than ActionScript 2.0 used in Flash Professional. Adobe's Flash Catalyst marked the peak of Adobe's investment in Flex, but its lack of popularity among its intended users was also a signal that interest in designer-developer use cases was not sufficient to sustain Adobe's investments in Flex.

While Adobe has used free and open source software and even placed parts of the platform under similar licenses, it has ultimately retained control of the keystones of the platform: the API and Flash Player itself. Paying browsers and operating system owners to include Flash Player left questions as to how the platform could be monetized compared to more traditional models of selling software or even of offering free software (such as a browser). If Macromedia had opened up the player and made its source freely available, that would result in the same divergence of implementations that led to the problems Flash sought to solve. The integrated solution was paramount, even as various competitors (Java, in particular, as well as JavaScript) experimented with different degrees of platform openness (see the appendix). The integrated solution was friendly to newcomers and amateurs because they did not need to know how every part of the runtime and browser interacted, only the abstracted layer on top.

Attitudes toward Ownership

Software fosters a sense of autonomy when the code is available. Knowing how an algorithm functions or the way a system accomplishes a task can inspire new solutions or ways to take advantage of that knowledge. This desire is behind the drive to make software's source "open" and move control of the means of production back into the hands of the user-programmer, who is almost always licensed software instead of sold it. Software licenses are a way to get around some of the constraints of sales, such as the first sale doctrine, where after a sale, the owner's interest is exhausted and the product can be lawfully resold, rented, destroyed, and so forth. Licensed software avoids this ownership issue entirely. The source code itself, however, can be licensed while still providing knowledge and insights into the working of the system. These "shared source" models are a compromise between control and the necessary understanding of the platform's inner workings.

There are many other reasons why a company or individual might want to "open" their source code beyond just providing a greater understanding of how it works. Reliability, reputation, volunteering, and even improvement through crowdsourcing development are just a few. Most new media artworks are not open source, though many tutorials described in chapter 3 are. This presents an interesting opposition. While the mechanics and even the aesthetics are free to emulate and imitate, to a degree, the ability to directly modify a program is relegated to add-ons to published games. The exception usually revolves around libraries, where the maintainers benefit either from a premium version (as in TweenLite, a library that provides functions to ease creation and management of programmatic tweens) or from support of the otherwise freely available software.

Having access to the platform's code can provide a new media artist insight into how the platform works, including ways to extend its capabilities. It can make modifications that use internal APIs or extensions possible; it even allows basic classes to be modified for a specific purpose, such as enabling a certain behavior. It can also allow a user to subvert the platform for artistic intent. This practice is common, though in object-oriented programming, extension of classes is done without access to the original code. Access to the source code is not always necessary to learn more about a platform, but it can help. Revealing source code can also open the door to critiques, just as the methods of critical code studies described by Mark C. Marino enable us to find biases and intention in the same way we might critically read any text (Marino 2006). The other side of the open source coin is the ability to contribute bug fixes, features, and changes, which Adobe only permitted through submissions without any guarantee of action or follow-up intervention.

Adobe released the specifications to the Flash Player virtual machine, but in stages and not as much as many had hoped. The Flex SDK included a fully functional compiler and the donation of Tamarin to Mozilla, including the source of the virtual machine itself. Adobe and Macromedia, though, withheld the key elements that make the platform as a whole work. For the Open Screen project, Adobe sought partners to help universalize Flash Player beyond desktop devices, but eventually closed applications (Adobe 2008). The reasons Adobe had for withholding the release of the full system under an open source license has two explanations. First, many parts may in fact not be owned by Adobe. That is certainly the case with the Sorenson video codec. Second, if the player was open sourced, a competitor (or even a well-wisher) could create an implementation and eliminate the uniformity of the platform. This would have almost certainly been carried out by someone within the open source community, and in fact was through the open source implementation of Flash, Gnash, in 2005 by John Gilmore:

> Gnash is based on the excellent work done on the public domain program "GameSWF," a graphics library for games that contains the heart of a Flash interpreter. Further development will aim this code toward the goal of playing arbitrary Flash "movies." This goal diverges from the goals of the GameSWF maintainers (which are to make a good public domain graphics library for games), and they were unwilling to accept some of our patches as a result. We're forking the code and pushing foward. New code for Gnash will be licensed under the GPL (version 2 or better). I'm sure we can contribute public domain bug fixes back to GameSWF, though our major development will be GPL licensed. (Gilmore 2005)

Lightspark (http://lightspark.github.io/) attempted a more optimized, hardware accelerated implementation, though it falls back on Gnash for AVM1 SWF files. The prevalence of Flash and the lack of an up-to-date, free player was seen as a direct threat against the free and open source ecosystem.

We'll revisit the events that surrounded the refocusing of Adobe's efforts, but one of the more significant contributions to open source occurred in November 2011. Adobe donated the software development kit (SDK), Flacon, and BlazeDS (a streaming media server) to the Apache Software Foundation (Adobe 2011). It no longer was a compelling case for Adobe to maintain itself. The community around it was no longer a large enough source of revenue to justify the maintenance of a large and complex library. Adobe dedicated a number of engineers to the project, however, and went to lengths to assure developers that it was not letting Flex go. But Flex was no longer being positioned by Adobe as a key property, even though it added value to the Flash ecosystem.

Co-opting Standardization

A standard in software helps advance related technologies by reducing the friction to integration. It can also stifle innovation or a more vertical integration by a single company. Standards in hardware include the Ethernet cable, known as RJ-45, while in software they include JSON (JavaScript Object Notation) and HTTP (HyperText Transfer Protocol). Technologies that either supplant or attempt to advance basic functions, like the Thunderbolt cable and Lightning port used in later Apple products, face opposition because they require users and manufacturers to invest in an additional ecosystem of ports, devices, and redundant cables in some cases. The lack of winning standards in hardware has consequences already familiar to those of us who carry around multiple devices, with a separate cable for each, knowing we will need a new charger for any new piece of technology that comes into the house. This lack of interchangeability gives the proprietor control at the expense of usability. Software standards are less functional; Adobe Photoshop is often named an industry standard for manipulation of images/pixels. Flash technologies are placed in opposition to "open standards," such as HTML5. The fact is Flash was considered by much of the industry as the de facto standard for interactive multimedia because of the sheer amount of content created and the lack of pervasive use and installation by its closest competitors, Silverlight and Java applets.

Flash's use of open standards is a marketing move: capitalizing on the practical benefits of a bazaar of developers while retaining key aspects of the cathedral. The "open standards" that Adobe refers to includes the language, the specification of the compiler, and the file format itself. To developers, and even hardware manufacturers, "open" is certainly more flexible and reliable. This perception is at odds with the reality of how a piece of software or hardware is open and what that openness depends on. The open source movement has developed massive software projects without the traditional developer hierarchy and motivations that created operating systems such as Windows. Much of modern computing owes a debt to Linus Torvalds and to the kernel he maintains, called Linux. But open source software projects, including many releases of the Linux operating system, often require a certain level of expertise to use. Flash Player, distributed and updated by many browsers, does not suffer from conflicting versions, and even its efforts at backward compatibility make for a smoother user experience. The Linux operating system has never taken off with the average computing user thanks in part to the barriers to entry, which are considerably greater than the installation and automatic updating of a controlled release operating system like Windows or Mac OS. The web is full of complaints about Windows, from security threats to poor user interface design, but the open source alternatives will likely never rise as the primary choice for the mass market due to that required effort. The fate of open standards without a proprietary bottleneck or dependency on the web, in the hands of developers, may yet play out differently.

Hardware platforms from the Atari 2600 and the Nintendo Entertainment System were created with the intention of absolutely controlling and profiting from creations on those platforms. The pricing strategy for the Microsoft Kinect platform for Xbox 360 was explained by Chris Eisler as one of ancillary revenue: "The ability to sell Kinect for Xbox 360 at its current price point is in large part subsidized by consumers buying a number of Kinect games, subscribing to Xbox LIVE, and making other transactions associated with the Xbox 360 ecosystem" (Eisler 2012). Nintendo and Apple both make the argument that a controlled system improves quality of applications. Their control over development licenses and app store submissions respectively stands in contrast to the less restricted system in place in the Google Play store. Nintendo has made strides to improve access to its traditionally closed platform, including a few notable successes such as the *Bit.Trip* series, as has Microsoft with its Xbox Live Arcade. In an interview on the topic of barriers to entry, Dan Adelman maintains that in order to be licensed to sell your game on their platform, you "have to have some experience making games, you have to be able to keep any confidential materials like dev kits secure and you have to form a company" (Nutt 2013). These requirements are in stark contrast to most of the amateur developers who do not seek a profit and would not form a company. It also sets up the space as a commercial rather than expressive marketplace: nearly all of the Flash works we've discussed throughout our study have been released at some point as free or nearly free on the web. Limiting a platform to commercial intentions cuts out some of the freedom to experiment.

However, Adobe's control of the Flash platform is exerted on several dimensions outside distribution. Adobe, like Macromedia before it, pays to have the player updated and included in operating systems and browsers—namely, Internet Explorer and Mozilla Firefox, who dominate the browser marketplace. Adobe also has provided technical details of parts of the platform, enough so that competitors have emerged in the authoring space even for its own player. Specifically, Adobe first released the compiler for Adobe Flex under the Mozilla Public License. This license, like others discussed later in this chapter, requires developers to contribute modifications to core source files if republished, but enables developers to extend and sell code free of any license fees. Adobe also maintains the only implementation of Flash Player that works fully, despite releasing certain components of the platform.

The Flash platform is comprised of numerous components and standards. A pure software platform, it still retains many similarities with a hardware platform, with the exception of the virtual machine that replaces the hardware that evolves and supports progressively more of the capabilities of the host systems. The entire platform can be decomposed into the VM, the language, the API, and the core libraries. The core library includes class definitions, such as those for the timeline, Stage, and DisplayObjects, as well as code that implements event handlers and manages the DisplayObject life cycle. The virtual machine itself implements features in native code, such as data structures and interactions with the host operating system or browser. The elements of the platform that were opened up included Macromedia's release of Flash 3's specifications in 1998. This was followed later by Adobe's release of Flex 3 (and a compatible compiler) in June 2007 under the Mozilla Public License. Later specifications that were relaxed include the RTMP (Real Time Media Protocol, used in the open source Flash Media server, Red5), and the AMF (ActionScript Message Format), a binary format that described a data object for communicating typed Flash objects. Adobe also donated Tamarin, the Actionscript Virtual Machine implementation, to the Mozilla Foundation on November 7, 2006. Tamarin implements ECMAScript 4.0 that ActionScript 3.0 is based on. Tamarin was donated just before the draft specification it implemented was rejected in favor of ECMAScript 3.1. Tamarin's donation marked another major step by Adobe to open up the platform, but its reception led to a very limited impact on the larger web community.

The debugger and most of the SDK itself were also included, though the virtual machine and other aspects of the SDK wasn't enough to implement a complete version of Flash Player. The availability of a freely available compiler enabled third-party development tools to compile code to SWFs and even modify the compiler for various purposes. One of the most prominent examples of a third-party tool developed specifically to produce Flash bytecode is FlashDevelop, a .NET-based ActionScript and Flex editor for Windows. Finally, the Flash C++ cross compiler, FlasCC, was contributed to open source as *CrossBridge*. The cross compiler uses the same LLVM as the iPhone: an ironic juxtaposition, given the fate of Flash on that hardware device.

Each of these milestones marks a moment in the platform's history when a component benefitted more from being available to developers than maintained exclusively in the developer community. Projects such as Red5 and osflash.org indicate a vibrant open source community that could contribute enhancements and bug fixes as required by the Mozilla Public License. The danger of providing all of the details of a platform's operation, of course, is that it would be incorporated as the output or product of a competing higher-level language, making the value of Adobe's revenue source, the development environment, obsolete.

One prominent example of a "write once, run anywhere" platform that incorporates a compilation to Flash option is Haxe: "If you could only learn one programming language, Haxe would be it. It's universal, it's powerful, it's easy to use" (Haxe 2013). The framework employs a source-to-source compiler that outputs JavaScript, ActionScript, C#, C++, and Java from a single language based on ECMAScript. It is also free and open source. Flash's forays into multiplatform deployment consist mainly of deployment using AIR. ActionScript libraries and code can be shared between Flash web applications and AIR applications on Mac, PC, and now almost all mobile platforms. Haxe represents a different approach, one that ignores specifications at a level lower than the language and instead relies on the availability of an appropriate output to a low-level virtual machine to finish the translation.

Technical capabilities and features are in a constant state of change in software platforms that release new versions as frequently as once a year, based on the current priorities of the competitive landscape. Thus any platform that is accepted by a community as a standard must be seen as advancing its capabilities and the interests of its users. Openness, with respect to a software platform, is the degree to which the stewards of a platform not only facilitate additional value systems to exist but also share that stewardship. That can involve granting control of the platform, or simply sharing the tasks of determining direction or features. Flash has sought out a relationship of codependence with its community of developers, adopting a combination of open source licenses and absolute control over a select (but critical) domain within the platform. Instead of a magical system that "just works," open source software can be an ongoing process unless properly curated for novice users.

Expansion

Flash was used in the later 2000s as a battleground in the war between Android and iPhone. Typically referred to as "the entire web," phones that could run Flash were touted as superior because of the large amount of Flash content still being produced and available on the web. In particular, Flash games as a genre had not yet been replaced by their HTML equivalents, both in quality and in diversity, by the time the iPhone had reached its third generation. But this was also an advantage to the app store approach: if free web games equaled the quality of games available on the store, then there wouldn't be any incentive to purchase. Flash's initial approach to the rise of mobile technology was to pursue opportunities through traditional channels: existing handset manufacturers who were unwilling to change the capabilities but offered access to the menus for application use (see the appendix). Nokia was one example where Flash applications were allowed access, though only through the more restricted Flash Lite format.

Flash was reaching into new markets in 2006, when AIR was first deployed. The idea was that this platform, which was increasingly being used for interface design, could be used for enterprise customers. It could be used either as a front end for a database system or as an ideal medium for rich Internet applications. Thus the tools that Adobe provided increasingly reflected increasingly high requirements to produce work with Flash. Even the title of the flagship artist-friendly application asserts its status as "Professional." Part of this trend accompanies the professionalization of the web; as digital distribution networks are increasingly corporate-owned and user-generated, content is simply part of the stream powering those web services (Twitter, Facebook, and YouTube all being prime examples). The gulf has widened between the Internet's haves (those with domain names and servers to host them) and the have-nots (those formerly residing, with its accompanying freedom and blank slate on Geocities, now primarily spread among a bevy of services such as LinkedIn, Facebook, and BlogSpot). Where personal sites once might have ranked high in the search results for a dedicated topic, the web now belongs to huge conglomerates, with user-generated content often residing in spaces controlled by a larger company who profits from freely produced work—a system not unlike Adobe's methods of profiting from openness while ultimately controlling Flash.

Macromedia and Adobe chose to open up parts of the platform in order to increase the prominence and ubiquity of content designed for their runtimes. Flash Player homogenized the differences between browsers and operating systems. Well before Adobe's release of AIR, a number of projectors that wrapped Flash SWF files were available to make it easier to sell and download Flash programs outside a web context. Up until Apple's resistance, Adobe was able to make the argument that it could overcome barriers for its developers. Flash video, including famously its use in YouTube, was one of the most popular uses for monetizing the technology; Hulu's streaming video service also used it for the digital rights management (DRM) and throttling. That was one of the inspirations behind the first version of Flex (which rendered Flash on the server) and the Flash Media server: by providing a service, Macromedia and Adobe could count on an ongoing revenue stream rather than depending on license sales to authoring tools (see the appendix). Developers used shareware locks, providing a trial version of a program and allowing the unlocked version to be purchased. This predicted the development and potential of AIR.

However, Adobe's attempts to market AIR never took off with a single distribution or sales network maintained by Adobe, despite being installed with Adobe Acrobat. Thus, once the framework was installed on a user's computer, there was no clear way to find other applications to take advantage of the technology. Instead, the applications were advertised and distributed through large companies like the New York Times or Pandora, who sold desktop versions of their services. This also removed opportunities for small companies to profit, as well as for Adobe to commandeer any share of profits on digitally released programs. The marketplace model, however, was not so well-established when Adobe entered the scene—mobile devices, with their limited access to traditional means of software installation, would spearhead the move toward marketplaces and a change in the economics of software.

A lack of a single marketplace for selling these applications prior to the AIR marketplace also stymied the general trust of AIR applications, as there was no clear authority certifying their identity—each application had to acquire a certificate or more often rely on users accepting the unknown application's installation. The concept of Internet-enabled application was plagued in the minds of its pioneers and even its users by its dark side: what level of access should websites or application creators have to a client? Recent cross-domain widgets such as Facebook's Like button and Google's +1 detect the user's logged-in status and update to reflect appropriate information, but they do so by launching a browser within a browser to ensure the security of their data from other scripts running on the same page. Allowing an application downloaded from the Internet to be seamlessly installed on the client as a native application raises warning bells for many users, thanks to the associations with Trojan horses and other malicious code. Prior to the rising popularity of digital distribution, this wouldn't have seemed a promising decision—and when amateur creators were involved, there was still reasonable suspicion associated with trusting a newly launched application.

Amateur and professional artists weren't the only ones affected by the choices of the Flash platform. Web developers, too, found the taste of freedom to release applications to the desktop enticing but at the same time restricted how far they could move those applications out of the browser. Using the web to distribute programs with the ease and convenience of visiting a web page was a significant step forward, but many at the forefront of exploring the boundaries of the platform wanted more.

Native Power

Adobe's quest to open up the web extended beyond the boundaries of its own plug-in. The debate on whether to allow an AIR application access to the underlying hardware or libraries is fundamentally political, and not technological, and is tied closely to its conception as a cross-platform Internet application. Flash's original constraints required its rendering pipeline to be optimized for use on the central processing unit (CPU), so even allowing access to the graphics processing unit (GPU), much less allowing arbitrary native libraries to be called from ActionScript, required significant rewriting of the codebase of the runtimes. The appeal of speed and power and the knowledge that they would maintain their advantage enabled Adobe to support access to hardware acceleration that enabled smooth 3D graphics, first through limited transformations of existing display objects in a "2.5D" manner and, finally, in Flash Player 11 with the low-level graphics API code-named Molehill and later christened Stage3D. The library translates code between the player and either OpenGL or DirectX, a feat that as of 2013 browsers with WebGL have not yet been able to achieve. Microsoft refused access for WebGL on Internet Explorer, considering direct access to the GPU to be a large security hole, which may limit any such applications in the future given IE's still impressive market share (Forshaw 2011).

The same questions of level of access are continually being addressed as web browser implement more and more native-like features such as local databases or access to the GPS (global positioning system). Interprocess communication is expensive. It's often avoided by more intensive applications because of the dangers of locking and synchronization. When one process is waiting for another to complete its work, the conflict could prevent the interface from responding to user input or a network resource from loading. The ability to launch or use other programs, however, is an expectation for a full desktop application, and this ranges from desktop widgets to programs that share data with other programs.

Children often play in sandboxes, a protected environment where falling usually is cushioned and the dangers are known. That is why the term has been adapted to mean a system that prevents danger to the surrounding system. This is achieved in browsers by limiting executable code from directly accessing the file system, but this also limits some of the abilities of web-downloaded programs. The decision to open the sandbox within which Flash Player operated to be capable of interacting with native applications was seen as a challenge. It would enable new types of applications. When AIR introduced the native process API, it conceded that users wanted to be able to launch a native application. Communication between that application and the original Flash application, though, could occur only through the standard in/standard out streams, usually reserved for text and console interaction, and was available only on the desktop. There were several challenges to implementing this in practice, however, including limiting communication to text. This led developers (and the evangelists themselves) to favor command line utilities that already only communicated via text, though the problems with interprocess communication and general lack of performance for anything data-heavy continued.

Ideally, cross-platform applications should be uniform in their capabilities, while native applications most certainly are not. Developers were clamoring for a new venue for their libraries and code, however, and the idea of extending the development tools into the desktop were compelling. Both Ed Rowe and Kevin Lynch, original members of the Apollo project, were worried that developers might target only a single platform with the native code required of such AIR application. There was a feeling that this sense of foreboding contributed to the decline in popularity of Shockwave, as Arno Gordoul, director of Adobe Flash Runtime, explained in our interview with him: "It was about putting a road bump. It wasn't a question of completely prohibiting it. It was a question of how easy or hard you make it for developers to do the right thing. The argument was that people who . . . were willing to scale that wall, but for developers who weren't that determined, they would be directed to the right thing" (Murray 2012). This fear was relevant to the platform's success, as much so as the developer's perception of the future of the platform. Without the interoperability, a user looking to download an AIR application without support for his or her environment was bound to be disappointed. Lynch had also experienced a falling-out with the Shockwave Player when it became the subject of balkanization among operating system–specific features. Thus, the question of whether to allow developers the ability to build custom native extensions was charged with the needs of the user-developer versus security and interoperability.

In 2010, there weren't many left who opposed the addition of native process access. Rowe had moved on, taking responsibility for a new project. It remained, however, to convince Lynch and his superiors. A number of teams working on projects within Adobe wanted access to the native APIs, and even requested that they be opened up for their use only, so as to ensure they would meet the proper cross-platform requirements. With the release of AIR 3.0, native extensions were finally incorporated, allowing AIR applications access to hardware drivers and libraries through ActionScript, which, if programmed, could provide a fallback for the functionality in ActionScript if the native implementation wasn't available.

The ability to call native functions from within the same process as the Flash application was critical, as was the addition of the capability to other profiles beyond the desktop: mobile devices and TVs could utilize their own native code mediated through an ActionScript API. But by the time Adobe released the feature, multiple competing frameworks such as PhoneGap and Sencha already supported native applications in the mobile space, using JavaScript as the intermediary. The native extension feature of AIR is one of the most significant developments of the platform, along with the packager for iPhone, which pushed the technology significantly further than it was originally intended and helped bridge the last gaps between the original purpose and the actual usages. But the timing was less than ideal, and ultimately it signified a shift from a singular platform tool chain to one that used ActionScript as an easy-to-develop authoring platform that outputs to other more successful platforms.

The Move Away from Desktop AIR

Adobe had proudly reported the dominance of the Flash plug-in as the "world's most pervasive software platform," and in 2009—two years after AIR was launched—Adobe claimed a 99 percent penetration of PCs. But the rise of mobile brought with it new challengers, and an increased and compelling interest in native web technologies was reflected even in the fate of some of AIR's early exemplar projects, among them TweetDeck. After acquisition by Twitter, TweetDeck underwent a transformation and consequently lost many of its other web service integrations in favor of a more exclusive focus. Yet the most essential reversal for TweetDeck came in 2011, with the total abandonment of AIR, as described by Lauren Dugan, former editor of AllTwitter:

> TweetDeck has also been moved over to HTML5, instead of Adobe AIR. This will come as a welcome change to anyone who was tired of the long startup times that AIR often experienced, and is a good sign for TweetDeck moving forward. However, the change means that TweetDeck's options have been limited: you can now download a

native app for Mac or Windows, a Chrome-based app, or a web client. (Dugan 2011)

The move indicates the strong allure of HTML5 but also acknowledges the relative limitations. The fact that it is a Chrome-based app signifies that standardization is still very much browser-specific, and thus any claim to "universality" is quite suspect. The change in the surface interface might not be dramatic, but the underlying infrastructure change impacts both the move to mobile and accessibility beyond the main operating systems.

Adobe's adopted strategy attempted to take advantage of the open source movement to grow the number of content creation programs as well as achieve a strong community of interest. Adobe moved through a progression of opening up first the specifications, then the language and other components of the platform. The value of the platform consisted of not only the universally updated runtime, but also the ease of development using the related technologies. Any content created for the runtimes would increase the value of the plug-in, so each level of openness increased the value of the system under Adobe's control.

When Flash's strategy met with resistance from Steve Jobs and Apple, developers who had spent years working with the Flash API realized that their skillsets based on ActionScript were in jeopardy. At the same time, the rise of alternatives monetization strategies also arrived, with the app store providing a unified, integrated solution outside the boxed software traditionally sold in physical stores. The app store provided a ready-made purchasing system for developers whose users had already entered their credit card information. For the web, models revolved around subscriptions and advertisements and even in cases like Amazon, micropayments. Such systems were hard to sustain with so much free content right alongside, and advertisers had an endless sea of options for casual games to support, making the return for any individual game maker likely low.

Not all of the changes in simplifying the purchase of software have been positive. Gay noted a general depression in software prices due to the large number of free applications. Even though software prices of boxed software were much higher and included the marketing, distribution, and the retail costs, they also set up an expectation of value. A similar expectation caused Adobe problems when it attempted to change its licensing terms after the latest shift to gaming and video.

Consolidation and Competition

After the expansion into Flex and AIR, Adobe realized that the expansiveness that was a strength was quickly draining resources compared to the return, especially in light of the multiple Flash Player tweaks necessary to keep the runtime consistent across different Android handsets and tablets. The consolidation began on November 9, 2011, when Adobe announced its focus consolidating on gaming and premium video (Winokur 2011). This included the ceasing of development of the Android Flash Player at version 11.2 as well as the donation of Adobe Flex to the Apache Software Foundation. The changes marked a major shift in outlook for the platform, including an outright proclamation that HTML was the future for web content.

In March 2012, Adobe announced the introduction of premium features to focus the contribution of the Flash ecosystem and to monetize it. These premium features included the Stage3D rendering, and primarily focused on the opcodes used to cross-compile games created using C/C++ to the Flash platform. These were used primarily by Unity. The terms are geared toward companies making large amounts of revenue: Adobe required 9 percent of revenue over $50,000. The introduction of the royalty system after a technology had been available for free, even under the conditions that left most amateur and smaller developers without the requirement to share revenue, caused a lot of resistance, especially as it occurred after Adobe's announcement of scaling back its Flash development. It was even called an "Adobe Speed Tax," since the feature was necessary for any game to be fast enough on the virtual machine (Cannasse 2012).

Based on feedback from developers, Adobe decided to change the licensing terms for the XC APIs and classify these capabilities as a standard feature. The XC APIs are no longer part of the Flash Player Premium Feature tier and do not require a separate license or royalties. Adobe rescinded the conditions on XC APIs only ten months later in January 2013 (Adobe 2013), also indicating that there were no longer any premium features. Unity announced after this move that it would be abandoning support for Flash output, for reasons of trust and the lack of commitment by Adobe: "By introducing, and then abandoning, a revenue sharing model, Adobe eroded developers' (and our) trust in Flash as a dependable, continuously improving platform" (Helgason 2013). Unity instead focused efforts on developing its own player, targeting Facebook developers and the Facebook platform in the same blog post. This marked a severe blow to any suggestion that Flash could remain dominant for online gaming.

Adobe's consolidation led to changes in the flagship Flash authoring tools as well. ActionScript 2.0 was removed as an option from the latest version of Adobe Flash, Creative Cloud, which was released in March 2013. This decision has sparked a number of indignant responses, mostly due to the widespread use of ActionScript 2.0 as an entry point into Flash. The majority of tutorials on the web are still written with ActionScript 2.0 in mind. Flex was further left behind with the release of a new Flash compiler, the ActionScript Compiler 2.0. The new compiler allowed for enhanced debug information and profiling, tools more of use to game designers attempting to tune high-end FPS games than amateurs creating their first platformer. Flash games have maintained their connotation but have expanded to include higher-end 3D games, including MMORPGs such as *Sacred Seasons* by Emerald City Games. The features Adobe introduced were in response to the innovative revenue models that developers were employing, primarily on Facebook but also on the Apple App Store. Whether Flash maintains its position as the standard for dynamic instant play web games remains to be seen, especially with the withdrawal of Unity output support.

Conclusion

Flash's attractiveness to creators is directly tied to its viability as a commercial product that achieves sustained usage. This is also true for hardware platforms. Developers regularly place bets on platforms released by big companies, positioning themselves as "launch" titles, or having fewer competitors among the platform's user base. By having a company such as Adobe dedicate resources to evolving, advancing, and otherwise maintaining the platform, developers can count on their works running on multiple browsers despite changes by the browser owners. Thus the story of Flash's relevance is directly tied to its openness and the balance between control and freedom. By attempting to exert too much control and expanding too rapidly, Flash lost its tenuous position as a de facto standard, due not only to developer's faith but also to development environments such as Unity abandoning support.

A truly open platform provides barriers to monetization and even audience, as any company who fully invests in it needs to cede control to the platform owner, even if it is a well-established company such as Microsoft or Apple. Unless communities organize around presenting works and solving the problems related to sales and distribution, the significance of the platform will erode. Unity, Haxe, and Flash have all staked out mobile beachheads to retain their relevancy to developers on modern platforms, but as a result they operate at the whim of the respective platforms, advancing their features to match and take advantage of their host. Apple, having absolute control over the iOS API and the distribution system for apps, possesses the ultimate keystone: its mobile architecture.

For Android, that centralized leverage is less consolidated but can be tied to the leading handset distributors, as application developers need to target a subset of the most popular hardware for resolution, processor speed, and capabilities.

Flash provides an example of a platform situated in very broad changes in the way users used it and the goals of the company who oversaw it. The choice to make the platform based on a standardized language (ECMAScript), along with opening up the specifications, could not guarantee Flash's success. The benefits in all cases were not enough to rescue the platform from Adobe's control at its critical moment. Adobe did not surrender more than control of the ebbing Flex SDK and instead increased efforts to transfer users of its software to its HTML5 authoring tools, as we discuss further in the next chapter on the future of Flash. The successful defense of Apple's platform and ecosystem from Flash Player's core value has paved the way to future closed platforms, despite being in the name of modern, open standards.

Introduction

Flash is dead. Long live Flash?

Variations of that headline, both despairing and gleeful, rang out around tech blogs all over the Internet: first in 2010, then with increasing assurance as the years passed, despite the failure of Flash to quickly exit the web. The 2010 announcement that started the early eulogies to Adobe's multimedia platform came from Steve Jobs, who offered his "Thoughts on Flash" and in doing so declared that Flash would not be supported on the iPhone or any future iOS device: "Flash was created during the PC era—for PCs and mice. Flash is a successful business for Adobe, and we can understand why they want to push it beyond PCs. But the mobile era is about low power devices, touch interfaces and open web standards—all areas where Flash falls short" (Jobs 2010). The condemnation by Jobs attacked Flash where it was weakest, as our examination of Flash's tenuous relationship with "openness" has noted, while also suggesting the ultimate failure for a software platform designed to adapt to any hardware system. Had Flash finally encountered hardware beyond the reach of its extension? Jobs's criticism suggested that Flash was now a relic of another time, the "PC era," and that that era was coming to an end—as such, Jobs seemed to be forecasting not only the end of Flash's hopes of colonizing the iPhone, but also the end of Flash's viability as a ubiquitous software platform. For years, Flash had sustained its ubiquity by outpacing the rest of the web. Now it seemed the web had finally outgrown it.

Did the iPhone and the many smartphones and tablets that followed really usher in a new era? Well, we typed this book on a desktop, and while you might be reading it on anything from an iPad to a Kindle to an actual printed page, it's likely your personal computer is not going anywhere. However, smartphones were only the beginning of Flash's downfall: the landscape of computing changed fundamentally. Jobs made his announcement while wielding the power of the iPhone, first released in 2007. The iPhone offered a perfect convergence between its music-inclined predecessor, the iPod, and mobile phones. For consumers, it was one device to carry instead of two, with an app-centered model of installable specialized programs, a web browser, and integrated wi-fi and mobile network support. Apple introduced the phone as "magic," with Jobs claiming: "iPhone is a revolutionary and magical product that is literally five years ahead of any other mobile phone. We are all born with the ultimate pointing device—our fingers—and iPhone uses them to create the most revolutionary user interface since the mouse" (Apple 2007). Its sleek touchscreen-only interface contrasted significantly with other cell phones of the year (such as the LG Voyager and Motorola Razr), which tended to be flip phones with physical keyboards and very limited access to the web through on-board browsers with minimal capabilities. Gaming on those phones was likely to be Snake or Tetris, and no one was yet clamoring to watch movies or cartoons on their tiny, low-resolution screens. The iPhone would change all that.

The Apple iPhone launched with Safari, a native browser with support for the fundamental structures of the web, including HTML, CSS, and JavaScript. However, the iPhone did not include any support for Flash, shutting out access to any of the works discussed throughout this book. This oversight was not surprising in the first generation of the iPhone, with its under-clocked 620 MHz CPU and minimal graphics processing power. However, even as the hardware grew more capable, Flash was locked out of the iOS mobile operating system and with it all content produced natively for Flash. Meanwhile, the number of smartphone options and users was growing. As of 2013, 56 percent of U.S. adults owned a smartphone—compared to 46 percent in 2012 and 35 percent in 2011—with a quarter of those users on iPhones (Smith 2013). The introduction of smartphones as platforms has certainly changed the landscape of life, with glowing screens a ubiquitous sight in every subway, on any street corner, in the hands of patrons at restaurants, and proffered to pacify children on long trips. With always-connected Internet access, the smartphone model theoretically places the web of "you" perpetually in everyone's hands, all the time. But this is the web without Flash: no smartphone even attempted to really support Flash until Google's Android Froyo operating system, announced in April 2010, just before Jobs made it clear with his "thoughts" on Flash that the Apple and Adobe rift was unlikely to ever be mended. Google's lead on Android development, Andy Rubin, noted the commitment to support Flash as part of Android's steps to be an open platform, while "not being militant about the things consumers are actually enjoying" (Stone 2010). The world of mobile was expanding, and Flash still had a spark left in its future—but the iPad, introduced that same year, threatened it even further. The iPad's larger display allowed Apple to market it as the ultimate device for content consumption, ushering in a next generation of portable web-browsing tablets without any support for Flash (Apple 2010). Likewise, the concept of apps and a closed marketplace offered a new outlet for the type of content that used to be found primarily in Flash arcades.

But while Flash's marketplace was completely free, without any intervention by Adobe beyond distribution of the plug-in, Apple had a different vision for the future of the web. Apple's restrictions include provisions based on content, which excludes apps such with "offensive" content—a term that invokes the definition of obscenity, "I know it when I see it," made famous by U.S. Supreme Court Justice Potter Stewart in 1964—a phrase used to justify decades of inconsistency and unfairly applied regulations on free speech. Would we expect any less of Apple? Consider the company's guidelines: "We review all apps to ensure they are reliable, perform as expected, and are free of offensive material. Before submitting your new or updated apps for review, check out the latest App Store Review Guidelines and Mac App Store Review Guidelines" (Apple 2013).

One of the most notable cases of a banned app came when a group of developers decided to offer a critique of Apple, and indeed of all smartphone manufacturers and users. This game shown in figure 7.1, *Phone Story*, was deemed to be offensive in its content and banned almost immediately after being approved—almost undoubtedly because it offered a direct critique of the Apple iPhone that cast the company in a decidedly unflattering and honest light. The developers then released the game on the web with an announcement that it had been banned from the App Store. The different levels of the game mimic traditional casual gameplay, not unlike the Flash newsgames we've discussed, and thus use play to effectively deliver the rhetoric of the argument. The story of the game makes the user complicit in the abuses of workers at every stage of the iPhone's production. To "win," the player must threaten children and catch suicidal workers jumping from windows and return them to their posts (Molleindustria 2011). Following the ban, designer Paolo Pedercini

Figure 7.1
Phone Story, 2011, Paolo Pedercini

explained, "The story was meant to generate some discussion about hardware and our socioeconomic impact as consumers of electronics, but now it's becoming more about market censorship" (Wortham 2011). This is a clear example of Noah Wardrip-Fruin's expressive processing, and the effective mechanism of delivery on the very device under critique is powerful. (The app is available on Google Play for Android phones, as another reminder that the restrictions placed by a platform can vary wildly.) On a platform like Flash, where distribution is in no way controlled by Adobe, this type of censorship would never be possible. Open distribution is essential to free expression—including the freedom to critique the very platform on which a work is released.

Adobe's choices had far-reaching implications for the platform's existing works and for media platforms in general. Flash attained the prized position as a de facto standard for dynamic interactive media, but Adobe's aspirations to be a pervasive platform required its virtual machine to be on all mobile platforms. Otherwise "write once, run anywhere" would turn into "write once, run in certain places." From a language and API perspective, the difference between a cross-compiled application and an applet running in a web browser is slight. The user experience of visiting the app store and the related processes and restrictions in place on apps in the app store make the applications significantly different. Jobs, in his critique of Flash, focused on the weakness of "write once, run everywhere" for matching a native system. Apple strives to maintain the brand's quality on its devices, and its Made for iPhone (MFI) program is a prime example of the care that it demands of partners in devices it endorses. For applications, Jobs insisted that any middle layer wouldn't be able to keep up with the pace of feature development. These qualities are much more subjective than a runtime trying to emulate native functions in a higher layer of abstraction. Apple has solidified its own choice for HTML5: a standard theoretically less proprietary, though notably in 2010 still emerging and not yet capable of truly replacing Flash. This decision held inevitable shades of a market-driven choice, as the lack of easy access to the existing interactive web on iPhones necessarily pointed users to Apple's walled garden, the App Store, for games and similar content.

Thus that moment of hope for Flash on mobile was short-lived. Adobe delivered the final announcement of the end of the mobile Flash Player in November 2011, ceding the terrain the platform had lost to its new rival, HTML5:

> Adobe is all about enabling designers and developers to create the most expressive content possible, regardless of platform or technology. For more than a decade, Flash has enabled the richest content to be created and deployed on the web by reaching beyond what browsers could do. It has repeatedly served as a blueprint for standardizing new technologies in HTML. Over the past two years, we've delivered Flash Player for mobile browsers and brought the full expressiveness of the web to many mobile devices.
>
> However, HTML5 is now universally supported on major mobile devices, in some cases exclusively. This makes HTML5 the best solution for creating and deploying content in the browser across mobile

platforms. We are excited about this, and we will continue our work with key players in the HTML community, including Google, Apple, Microsoft, and RIM, to drive HTML5 innovation they can use to advance their mobile browsers.

Our future work with Flash on mobile devices will be focused on enabling Flash developers to package native apps with Adobe AIR for all the major app stores. We will no longer continue to develop Flash Player in the browser to work with new mobile device configurations (chipset, browser, OS version, etc.) following the upcoming release of Flash Player 11.1 for Android and BlackBerry PlayBook. (Winokur 2011)

While this press release framed the rise of HTML5 in a positive light, promising a future for Flash on the desktop with increasing support for high-definition video and 3D graphics, many users read it as the final nail in the coffin of Flash. Can a universal platform reinvent itself as hardware-specific without serious consequences to its influence? Of course not. The mobile Flash platform's zenith could be arguably considered when it was used as the differential factor in the marketing war between Android and iPhone for best smartphone. As soon as Adobe announced its decision to cease development of mobile Flash, it was a surrender of its stated ambition to control a ubiquitous platform. This was the point where popular opinion truly changed; those developers who had been wagering that Adobe would prevail in its ambition for Flash to serve as a universal platform were sorely disappointed. The outpouring of emotion was prolific, including a page directly attacking Flash (http://flashsucks.org/). Additional websites were claimed to be "Flash Killers," proffering challenges to the incumbent (Falcon 2013). Flash's evolution from de facto standard to specialized authoring environment was shaped by the mind share and faith of its developer community and ultimately stood on the commitments and prospects of its stewards, and its fall was likewise characterized by their withdrawal of that faith.

Flash's defining affordance was its market penetration: universal, near-instant access through web-equipped devices was necessary to sustain its viability for developers of any website where Flash would be heavily featured or integrated into the interface. It is no surprise that many people read this announcement as the final nail in Flash's coffin: ZDNet's Steven J. Vaughan-Nichols lead with the headline "Flash is Dead. Long live HTML5," asking "Do you really think that desktop Flash will survive for long?" (Vaughan-Nichols 2011). Adobe employee Mike Chambers came forward to clarify the announcement, pointing out that Flash was still moving forward—but also reminding fellow members of the Flash community that change was inevitable:

> If a Flash feature is successful, it will eventually be integrated into the browser, and developers and users will access it more and more via the browser and not Flash. With the renewed competition in the browser market and the subsequent acceleration of new HTML5 features being added to browsers, the number of things possible in the browser has dramatically increased. This includes a lot of overlap with features that were once exclusive to the Flash Player. While it will still be a while before HTML5/CSS3 features have the same ubiquity as the Flash Player currently has, the trend is very clear. A lot of the things that you have done via Flash in the past will increasingly be done via HTML5 and CSS3 directly in the browser. (Chambers 2011)

We've noted this progression previously: Flash offered an easy solution for constantly pushing the boundaries of web interactivity, but it never went unchallenged as a platform for long. By setting expectations for how the web worked, Flash pushed at foundational web standards (including HTML and CSS) until they too evolved, by necessity rising as platforms for games, animation, and more. This integration of features could conceivably make Flash irrelevant, even on the desktops where Flash has already an established part of the browser ecosystem, thanks in part to security risks and the problems faced by a not-quite-open platform as chronicled in chapter 6. The security risks of Flash are not exclusive to Flash. Any browser plug-in can serve as a venue for cyberattacks, particularly when users ignore the many regular updates that both Java and Flash launch in response to the discovery of exploits. Efforts to maintain an increasingly draining set of Flash Player implementations on the many Android variants that it needed to focus on the forefront of Flash's capabilities, including "advanced gaming" and "premium video" (Winokur 2011). Flash's response, including this expansion of 3D and other capabilities more associated with traditional software, may yet be integrated into the browser too quickly for Flash to ever establish another unique feature, rendering Flash a legacy software platform, valuable primarily for experiencing the web as it once was.

But our study of the Flash platform is not yet a requiem. According to a 2013 Pew Survey, 70 percent of U.S. residents have broadband access at home, with an additional 10 percent accessing high-speed Internet only through their smartphones (Zickuhr and Amith 2013). Flash content is still readily available across the web to all with Internet access with the exception of those 10 percent on smartphones only, and Flash developers are still working. User development communities remain active. Newgrounds is still home to new submissions every day, and new conversations on the Flash forum addressing everything from the most recent version of ActionScript to working with keyframes and MovieClips are posted regularly. YouTube's desktop version launched an opt-in HTML5 trial, but still relies on Flash as a primary technology. Flash is still installed on nearly every desktop browser, and Flash production continues. Hulu and other premium video sites (excluding Netflix, which relies on Silverlight) still depend on Flash for controlling proprietary video content. But the signs of diminishing influence are there. In Adobe's Creative Cloud, a subscription software model introduced in 2013, both Flash Builder and Flash Professional have been relegated to the "also included" list rather than featured alongside headliners like Photoshop, Illustrator, and InDesign. Even the marketing of Flash focuses on the development tool's potential to port content to other platforms, with the inclusion of the Toolkit for CreateJS: a translator for using the primary capabilities of Flash to create HTML5 content (Shankland 2012). Essentially, this type of translation separates the development features of the Flash environment from its release platform, allowing users from the Flash community to leverage their existing development knowledge toward creating HTML5 content.

In light of this slow reduction in Flash's influence, and the many decisions on Adobe's part that demonstrate an acceptance of the inevitability of the degradation of Flash as a viable platform, it is not surprising that Flash has been hailed as dead even as fragments of the platform are very much alive. Development courses in Flash are gradually disappearing from university curricula (we dropped ours in favor of HTML5 around the same time as the mobile announcement), and there's no driving motivation aside from ease of mastery for new developers to pick up Flash as a platform. However, Flash Player remains a standard part of any desktop browser experience—though this too may change, and not just thanks to attempts to render Flash irrelevant by projects such as the Google Chrome Experiments. An online manifesto at Occupy Flash calls for a "movement to rid the world of the Flash Player plugin," arguing:

Flash Player is dead. Its time has passed. It's buggy. It crashes a lot. It requires constant security updates. It doesn't work on most mobile devices. It's a fossil, left over from the era of closed standards and unilateral corporate control of web technology. Websites that rely on Flash present a completely inconsistent (and often unusable) experience for a fast-growing percentage of the users who don't use a desktop browser. It introduces some scary security and privacy issues by way of Flash cookies. Flash makes the web less accessible. At this point, it's holding back the web. (Occupy Flash 2013)

The rhetoric is extreme, almost ludicrous. Clearly, the site is humorous (and has a corresponding parody site, Occupy HTML), but it is also a reminder of how difficult it is for a platform to really be abandoned. After all, artists, game creators, and animators have worked with old versions of Flash development tools quite happily for many years, and Adobe's gradual withdrawal from the platform is unlikely to impact many of their books on using Flash, such as Chris Georgenes's (2014) *How to Cheat in Adobe Flash CC*, which promises to support creators looking to make "an animated short, catchy and fun mobile game, or an innovative application," continue to hit the marketplace. A software platform of the scale of Flash cannot suddenly fade from the web, as it is integrated into the underlying architecture. Short of an unlikely successful conclusion to the Occupy Flash movement's call for the widespread abandonment of Flash Player, Flash content appears secure thanks to the platform's legacy.

Preserving Flash

At the 2014 Modern Language Association, Mark Sample's panel on "Electronic Literature after Flash" cites the death of Flash: "Flash is dying. And with it, potentially an entire generation of e-lit work that cannot be accessed without Flash. The slow death of Flash also leaves a host of authors who can no longer create in their chosen medium. It's as if a novelist were told that she could no longer use a word processor—indeed, no longer even use words. Or is it?" (Sample 2013). With that provocation, the panel ended with a reminder from Stuart Moulthrop (creator of *Pax* and other electronic literature works, as addressed in chapter 5) that Flash offered a way to develop "interesting interfaces" and thus enabled a style of art that will continue without Flash (but perhaps still with Flash's legacy of influence apparent.) Meanwhile, Dene Grigar and Stuart Moulthrop addressed the more urgent concern of preserving early works in an accessible form, with the help of an NEH start-up grant for the "Pathfinders" archive project (Grigar and Moulthrop 2013). Some options for preservation are already being explored within the electronic literature community: the Remixworks and Dreaming Methods collectives are preserving and sharing (for a fee) source files. This preservation is not just passive: it's also a conversation driven by "re-shaping each other's works, artistically discovering latent content in images, interfaces, animation, and other aspects" (Flores 2013). This style of preservation is appropriately avant-garde, with the remix rather than the static work perhaps living on.

The problem of preservation extends well beyond works that count on Flash as an expressive medium, though there is much in common with games. When a software's original owner has stopped maintaining it, users are forced to transition to other platforms. In older games, this is called abandonware, and the enforcement of copyright is often lax because the original authors are usually no longer receiving compensation for that piece. Jonathan Gay, in an interview by Arthegall referencing *Dark Castle* and several other abandonware titles he's worked on, implied that if an owner leaves his or her post, then the work should be freed: "If the creator is no longer interested in selling and maintaining their product, I think that it's very appropriate for the software to go to the public domain, and the creator should be grateful to people taking over the creator's rolls of keeping it alive. The value of software and information is in the combination of creation and use" (Arthegall 2012). Flash is still far from being abandonware, but it is a proprietary platform, with Adobe's control over the primary development environment and player giving them some ultimate saying power in its fate. This dependence on Adobe can be anxiety-inducing for members of the development community, particularly when Adobe's choices diverge from what users would like to see. Flash may demonstrate moments of user-driven evolution, but much is dictated in the top-down hierarchy of traditional software production.

Throughout this book, we've looked at many works of Flash spanning the past decades, available online thanks to the efforts of their creators and to communities that act as living archives of Flash creativity. However, that promise falters if Flash Player ever loses its place as a standard part of the ecosystem—or if Jobs's vision of a post-desktop world comes to pass, with most mobile devices no longer supporting Flash. The challenges of the digital preservation of Flash works is part of a larger problem of the ephemerality of software, although Flash's relatively constant presence in browsers has allowed it to escape the dangers of operating system changes or hardware changes in graphic acceleration that can render desktop software inoperable or at best difficult to use. The backward compatibility of SWF files (and, mostly, of Flash project files for editing) has promised an enduring access to Flash content. As long as the player survives, the content is still accessible, even if it is eventually frozen in a static and inalterable state thanks to more limited support by the development software itself. This was achieved by including the original virtual machine when the advances in the language necessitated an entirely new virtual machine. Thus, even on modern browsers, Flash Player can run content from the late nineties. The most dramatic leaps forward in the Flash platform were likewise complicated by faithfulness to the old elements, as with the preservation of the timeline alongside object-oriented controls, often leading to built-in redundancy of commands to support legacy programs. With the new changes to Flash Professional, including the introduction of HTML5 into even the Flash developer ecosystem, it is hard to predict how much longer the Flash development tools will support altering the source files of older content.

While these issues of playability and access are strong concerns for the preservation of Flash as a user-based (if not developer-driven) platform, Flash works also face the challenges all web-based works must confront, as their storage and accessibility is often entirely dependent on the sustained interest and the support of the creator or the release community. Putting something online guarantees that it is accessible, but only for the length of time of the hosting. Entire networks dedicated to user-generated, highly individual content creativity and experimentation have vanished from the web: free hosts like Geocities, Angelfire, and Tripod once offered quick solutions but eventually shut down, leaving orphaned sites and only a fraction of content preserved in online archives. With no one left to maintain them, even those sites still accessible become graveyards of broken links, dead scripts, and missing style sheets. The Internet Archive has preserved pieces of the web over time, but many more sites have been launched only to fade into obscurity after their developer lost interest or ceased paying for hosting space. As of 2012, the Internet Archive had saved over eighty terabytes of web data for research, noting that the content includes "any media that we were able to capture, including images, flash, videos, etc." (Internet Archive 2012). The Internet Archive Team's project represents one of the most extensive efforts of this kind; however, much more has been lost than preserved. For platform studies, and any attempt to examine more than the current surface of the changing body of the World Wide Web, this problem of access to works throughout the life of a platform is always going to be a limiting factor in the depth of study possible for web-based media. These limitations will further restrict research in fields such as media studies, game studies, and cultural studies where the ephemerality of potentially significant data can be frustrating. The problem of the incomplete record haunts software studies, and, in the case of something as big as the Flash platform, means any study will necessarily be incomplete.

Meanwhile, the transformation of hardware and the inescapable evolution of operating systems and web browsers might yet render Flash

Player antiquated, leaving orphaned files across the web. This recalls the challenges of older hardware platforms (as Bogost and Montfort observed in their study of Atari [Montfort and Bogost 2009]): not only is software lost, but it is rendered unplayable except for those who preserved the system or those playing on emulators. The emulation of Flash is already beginning—creators of art games are seeking to rewrite their code to use the same resources in HTML5, YouTube is experimenting with HTML5 access, and efforts such as Google Chrome Experiments are looking to prove HTML5's suitability for everything from re-creating Angry Birds to creating 3D dinosaur shooters. This cycle of emulation recalls the many attempts of Flash developers to build their own versions of Mario and other ported games: a platform used to imitate fading hardware may itself be fading. Even emulations of old hardware built in Flash software might themselves require preservation, or another layer of emulation, to remain viable. The Google Chrome Experiments are also a reminder of how quickly the status quo of the web can change. Google introduced the Chrome browser in 2008, when the browser market was dominated by Internet Explorer with 72 percent of the market, with Mozilla Firefox a distant second at 20 percent (Rosenblatt 2013). Chrome grew in viability in part by focusing on optimizing the browser as a platform. As Sundar Pichai, the vice president in charge of Chrome, explained: "We realized that for us to really drive applications, you need a great platform underneath, and in some cases deep integration with the hardware underneath . . . for us the underlying platform was the browser, and having a say there was very important" (as quoted in Rosenblatt 2013). The Google Chrome Experiments, with their focus on pushing HTML5, CSS3, and JavaScript to their max, demonstrate the browser's viability as a platform to rival Flash for interactivity.

What is responsible for Flash's fall from grace as a dominant platform for the future web? Blaming Apple's ecosystem (and their protectiveness of the app store as an exclusive market for games on iOS devices, without any competition from Flash arcade sites) is easy, but simplistic. The ubiquitous extension for the web bridged operating systems without a challenge, but those operating systems tended to be installed on fairly similar hardware. A Macintosh desktop may have different capabilities than a Windows PC desktop, but both share the keyboard and mouse, along with physical monitors whose scale and resolution changed at a relatively similar rate. On the other hand, the new hardware that Jobs heralded as the future eliminated the keyboard except as an occasional onscreen accessory, did away with the mouse entirely, and reduced screen size significantly while also transforming the user's context for interaction and with it expectations for use of sound. What can we learn from the dramatic consequences of new hardware to a platform grounded in software?

Certainly, the need to accommodate new hardware places demands on software platforms to continually evolve while maintaining the legacy of the past in their virtual DNA: the backward compatibility that keeps all dependent programs running. Hardware rarely drops out of nowhere, as it too evolves. The problems of compatibility with Apple and smartphones did not emerge out of nowhere any more than did the iPhone itself land without predecessors. The iPhone was the realization of ideas already rampant in science fiction, as seen everywhere from *Star Trek* to Isaac Asimov's 1964 article "Visit to the World's Fair of 2014," which included the prediction "You will see as well as hear the person you telephone. The screen can be used not only to see the people you call but also for studying documents and photographs and reading passages from books" (qtd. in Goss 2013). The decreasing scale of computers and processing hardware alone foretold a future of more powerful portable devices, although the use cases and demand for such hardware hadn't yet been established. The iPhone started a revolution, in part because it brought together a set of affordances previously scattered, and it united those advances in one eco-system. Flash's transformation of influence in the wake of the iPhone speaks to the centrality of hardware decisions in the life of a platform—even fundamentally multi-platform software. In our interview, Jonathan Gay noted how mobile was on the radar for a long time, before the era of smartphones truly brought web capabilities to mobile. However, he explained that the early limitations of the "horrific and slow" browsers, with limitations imposed by the phone manufacturers and operators, made it unfriendly to any technology—including Flash.

Faced with these constraints, Flash's developers tried to compensate by building a reduced version of the platform specifically for mobile. However, just as the constrained browser ultimately proved unusable, any attempt to reduce Flash for mobile would be hindered by the need to make obsolete old content or limit the power of ActionScript 3—ultimately resulting in a separate platform, not the cross-platform solution that Flash needed to retain viability in an increasingly mobile market. The expansion of hardware power and speed on the desktop corresponded with a growth in Flash features. But that complexity came at the cost of the original scale of Flash: as Gay told us, "Flash was very lightweight originally. But over time people were developing content for these fast PCs; who cares if it takes 30MB to render this Flash movie, look what it does!" When faced with mobile, those strengths became weaknesses, as noted by Jobs in his explanation for Apple's parting of ways with Adobe on mobile: "Flash is a cross platform development tool. It is not Adobe's goal to help developers write the best iPhone, iPod and iPad apps. It is their goal to help developers write cross platform apps. And Adobe has been painfully slow to adopt enhancements to Apple's platforms" (Jobs 2010). The lack of hardware specificity now marked Flash as a monolithic solution to increasingly particularized challenges of development: a "one-size-fits-most" platform that no longer represents the best solution to any task. The same feature-creep that spread through the platform as it responded to the needs of animators, game developers, website designers, and other users made Flash unwieldy for mobile.

When Jobs offered his thoughts on Flash, he advocated for replacing it with what he called more modern, open standards: HTML5, CSS, and JavaScript. These are familiar names, and not really modern at all. Discounting the "5" at the end of HTML, the web has circled back to the same fundamental structures that preceded Flash, but the affordances of these platforms now reflect many of the same capabilities Flash used to enhance. While ActionScript is a relatively complete programming language (as defined by Turing completeness, or the ability to express any computational expression, as Florian Cramer explored), HTML and other markup languages are incomplete (Cramer 2008). The continued extension of JavaScript and the reworking of HTML standards is making the web's fundamental technologies more "complete" within themselves, in part in an attempt to eliminate the need for scaffolding of the kind that Flash provided, partially aided by the contributions of Adobe—the affordances of Flash became the affordances of the web, provided by native technologies and without the need for accepting installation of browser extensions.

Comparing Flash and HTML5

However, the years of development of the Flash platform, and particularly its development tools, cannot be ignored when examining this new status quo. HTML5 likewise has a long history: the first HTML standard was created in 1990 in a (somewhat futile) attempt to bring web browsers onto the same page in their interpretation of the web's structure. (The difference between browsers and their presentation of HTML and CSS continues, complicated in part by the addition of proprietary tags and readings to the HTML base.) Over the years of revision, the HTML standards fragmented: new variants and markup languages such as XHTML, DHTML, and XML gained followings by offering extensions aimed at enabling interactivity and animations, demonstrating the need for components that would be integrated into HTML5. The World Wide Web Consortium announced the definition of the HTML5 standard at the end of 2012, with CEO Jeff Jaffe noting the following: "The broader the reach of Web technology, the more our stakeholders demand a stable standard . . . as of today, businesses know what they can rely on for HTML5 in the coming years, and what their customers will demand. Likewise, developers will know what skills to cultivate to reach smart phones, cars, televisions, ebooks, digital signs, and devices not yet known" (W3C 2012). Jaffe emphasizes the devices of the future—the Achilles' heel of the Flash platform in its trajectory, and a reminder that decisions made by hardware manufacturers can ultimately dictate the fate of any software platform. But these are promises as of yet unfulfilled: as a platform for animation and game making, HTML5 is still limited. The lack of clear proprietary ownership of HTML5 means that there are many competing tools, particularly libraries that duplicate functionality, for development, unlike the Adobe-led world of Flash development—a circumstance that means there are a variety of tools for developing HTML5, which can be both an advantage and a disadvantage to a platform's utility. No one tool or library has the level of documentation or community support that Flash has acquired over the years, though time might push a dominant model to the top of the HTML5 heap.

Working directly with HTML5 is entirely scripting-based, and is only translated to visual once rendered. One direct analogue to the visual space of Flash is in HTML5's addition of the Canvas element, named to evoke the creative metaphor of a blank artist's space. Canvas offers pixel-by-pixel control of a designated space in a browser window (or the entire browser screen), with a series of drawing tools for adding vector objects, paths, image files, text, and other objects onto the screen. The Canvas baseline standard only understands Canvas as a blank slate reminiscent of a single frame of Flash: there is no attempt to build an understanding of time or objects as defined and trackable within the current standard, as HTML continues to provide primarily structure while Javascript handles the interactivity (W3C 2013). SVG is another alternative adopted in HTML that closely resembles the vector format used in Flash, but situated within the HTML object framework. While the beginnings of moving paths, transformations of pixels, and changeable content are present, the addition of extensive coding or the use of scripting libraries is essential to Canvas's effectiveness. Among those, there are several that advertise themselves as comparable to Flash. The EaselJS library promises "an API that is familiar to Flash developers, but embraces Javascript sensibilities" (CreateJS 2013). The demos for EaselJS demonstrate replicas of interactions familiar to any Flash site visitor: drag and drop, filters, vector masks, object transformations, image transformations, and mouse interactivity.

As of the end of 2011, Adobe announced both the end of their efforts to develop Flash for mobile and their intention to focus on HTML5 through several new products in their Edge series. One of these development tools, Adobe Edge Animate, is reminiscent of Flash's timeline and offers many of the same metaphors for keyframes and tweening at the heart of Flash as an animation tool. The back end may have changed significantly, and the final produced animation is integrated directly into a web-ready HTML file, but alongside the changes to Flash Professional the Edge development tools offer a clear glimpse of Adobe's vision of the future of the web. The Edge Animate program is even marketed as a tool to "create animated, interactive content for the modern web"—the emphasis clearly promising that Adobe does not want to be counted out of the HTML5 revolution, even if they can no longer control the underlying platform (Adobe 2013). HTML5 is here to stay, at least until new hardware and unforeseen requirements push the web on to the next "big thing" or the web itself evolves.

Legacy of a Software Platform

When Lev Manovich noted the aesthetic changes the web was undergoing at the hands of the experimental "Generation Flash," he made sure to note that Flash wasn't the only platform for the works he examined. Flash's impact on the web transcends the software of its development tools, and even the file structures of SWF and the many scattered works cannot contain Flash. Much of the current experimentation with HTML5 involves replicating the affordances of Flash—and while that is only a starting point, it demonstrates how integral Flash's legacy is to shaping expectations of web content development. The current movement away from Flash is not an abandonment of the platform. Flash developers are not rats abandoning a sinking ship: they are professionals and dedicated amateurs bringing their skill sets and expectations to everything from developing for the cross-platform web to building dedicated software or mobile applications. The integration of Flash-like qualities in solutions for HTML5 built by Adobe and open source communities suggests that the underlying Flash philosophy is here to stay, and many of the Google Chrome Experiments are Flash-like in their interfaces. While Manovich's Generation Flash may now be all grown-up, those same developers who learned and honed their art in the days of Flash may well be building the affordances and scripting methods of the next big software platform.

Throughout this book, we've profiled the Flash platform as it evolved from a simple tool for animation to a complex object-oriented environment for developing interactive multimedia. We've surveyed only a small sampling of the works from the many genres of Flash under study here: animation, games, new media art, Internet applications, and the many pieces that make up multimedia websites. All of these genres existed to some extent before Flash, but Flash has been pivotal in reinterpreting them for the web. Even the hardware devices such as the iPhone that have rejected Flash support in their operating system still run programs originally created in Flash, ported through the app store and repackaged for the new marketplace. Software platforms must be approached holistically, but the works they produce are not necessarily trapped in their own ecosystem. Just as Flash works appeared on television and in galleries, so too will Flash-produced creations continue to show up in unexpected places, perhaps rendered unrecognizable and viewed without using Flash Player or opening a SWF file. Communities like Newgrounds might be reinvented, or disappear and leave a vacancy for some new creative exchange to fill, but the tools that power them can only get better and more accessible. And those new tools will be shaped by the affordances Flash developed over nearly twenty years of evolution. As a platform, it encouraged subversion: Adobe's courting of openness invited a continual reshaping, and the freedom inherent in how Flash projects were originally distributed enabled it to become a medium for critique and controversy. The precedent Flash works set will continue to inspire innovations in games, animation, and interactive art. The legacy of Flash, and most importantly the vision of a dynamic and interactive web, will outlive both Flash development tools and Flash Player. Without Flash, we wouldn't have a "modern web." Flash may die someday, but the web will be resplendent with Flash's progeny: animation, casual games, new media art, and even a few new emulators for revisiting the platform's legacy.

Appendix: An Interview with Jonathan Gay

JM: What was the first commercial influence on the technology? What compromises/decisions were made early on?

JG: The main constraint was our time and not understanding what the problem was. Do we put sound in the first version, what kind of features? Initially we built a drawing package that influenced a lot of things, but wasn't a product for the Internet. And then we said, well, we have drawing, let's add animation to it. There weren't a ton of choices, it was more gradual: How do we build it, what do we put in next? What's the most important thing: what do we build next?

Mac user editors, early users. We really need a button in it. If we just had a button. The interactivity wasn't in the original design, it was the animation.

JM: What is your feeling toward the developer amateur/creator divide? Was this designed for amateur?

JG: Early on, identifying the key audience was the innovation. Used to be you had an artist doing media, then you'd hand off to the programmer to do the programming. That was a pretty inefficient process. Do media in Illustrator/Photoshop, and we were differentiated. We started out with the artist, and they sort of gradually got into programming—at least early on, where one person could do the whole project. And that was a unique thing. Gradually as the project got more sophisticated, then it went back to a more specialized model where you had a developer doing the program-ming and working with assets from artists. Being able to blend that world was interesting from a platform perspective.

JM: Did you find some of the early decisions not being ideal? Especially with the differences between AS2.0 and the original ActionScript.

JG: Yeah, that was the motivation behind the redesign of the api and programming models. It started with a drawing package and an animation package, so it was difficult to have an elegant evolution. I was also getting less involved in the project at that point, but trying to make a cleaner abstraction. Another thing that was different about it from a platform perspective, and it wasn't a super pure thing, but compared to building a Mac application, there wasn't a discrete line between the content and the controls. Being able to describe the interactive elements between the platform instead of a set of pre-canned UI elements. That was definitely a challenge, to find the right level of abstraction.

JM: Some of the earliest metaphors of stage and characters, it really made it easier for some people to grapple with these ideas of moving images and adding behaviors to images. It's embedded in some of the core DNA of the stage. Can you talk about the evolution? How did you come up with those early choices of terminology in the programmer interface?

JG: There's this question when you're developing a project. In the early stages, you just want to draw it, build the prototype. Then you implemented it. Flash was unusual in that you could take that initial drawing in the prototype and gradually add behavior to it. Whereas a lot of other things are you do the prototype and the programmer goes off and figures out the right structure. Flash wasn't programming by example, but some of the design ideas were inspired by oh, if you just program by example.

An earlier project I did was IntelliDraw. Sort of like Visio, almost a competitor to Visio. The idea is you do you drawing and then you add behavior to it. So that definitely influenced Flash. That was why some of the artists were able to become programmers, because they could start with it and gradually add behavior.

JM: Do you find that surprising or a consequence of giving these capabilities to people and providing a pathway to realizing them?

JG: The first surprising area, early on, before we had ActionScript, someone built a pinball machine in Flash. It was a state machine where they had a bunch of frames and tell targets, and if you clicked the button at the right time, then it would go branch off that. This person was insane. It was an artist who wanted a pinball machine. It was a little bit of logic and a lot of states out there. Once I saw that, nothing surprised me.

Certainly the aspiration with Flash was to be general-purpose. Let's make it as general-purpose as we can. It was one of the early platforms to use vector graphics and user interfaces, so we were thinking, "Let's leverage that" to make a general-purpose platform.

JM: At what point did you realize this was a platform, even before the term became popular in describing it?

JG: It was a gradual realization. There are different ways to define platform. Macromedia acquired Flash pretty early on; we were sitting as the little kid next to Director hoping not to get canceled. It was a gradual realization: "Wow, they have this developer community. This is an amazing thing. You have these people who have all these mental structures about how to use your tool. And the things they do inspire other people and there's this positive feedback loop. And they make money building this stuff." To me, that's the key part of the platform: when you have this community around it, and they are doing things, and they are adding value on top of it, they become invested in it. We saw it in developers first, and "Wow, it looks as if Flash is doing that, too."

JM: Flash and Director were similar in output. Could you talk a bit more about those feelings, being acquired by Macromedia?

JG: We were pretty much just focused on building the product, so it wasn't a huge impact. Macromedia insulated teams a little bit. Yeah, there was definitely some intensive competition. Whose space is this? Let the marketplace decide. Director was an older project, it was really designed for CD-ROMs. The problem was, what do I do with these 300 MB or whatever it was? People were trying to build big content, and that evolution made it harder to make the transition. It's just as if Flash didn't make the transition on mobile.

JM: How did the early decision of the loading first of SWFs come about? This is very different than JavaScript.

JG: The original inspiration was that we wanted to have an animation start playing before it was fully loaded. And we wanted it to be as small as possible, so using a dictionary approach where you have a set of assets, and it's almost a compiler as you generate the SWF, where it's figuring, "What frame do I need these assets on? Okay, I'm going to put this shape here, this font here and this sound here, and once it's there, I'll use it." It just evolved from that.

One of the early animations was this goofy thing; we had this artist who had a seal and he was bouncing a ball. That was a big deal; it's like, could you make the seal start moving as quickly as possible? You want to look for the optimal solution. And so the optimal solution was just send the media you need for that frame and reuse it as often as you can.

JM: We're looking at Flash's role in finding the balance between open and proprietary. I've looked at the encoding issues, as well as Flex's contribution to Apache. Is there an original idea of how much of the platform should be open, especially in light of the Linux community's requirements and more stringent requirements?

JG: It's certainly a complex set of issues. My perspective when I was working on Flash and helping run it, was that we were stewards for the community. We also wanted to get paid too, but it was like, what was the right thing to make sure people can build content and have it play where they need to have it play? The question of what level of openness was appropriate is one that was a continual question for a while. Should we open it up, should we not? Even if we opened it up, what would someone do with it? Would they just build an authoring tool? Would there be someone who would have a separate implementation of the player? IT could certainly start to get pretty complex. You saw with the browsers how hard that was. So it seemed as if that wasn't really practical. It wasn't a religious thing, it was what was the pragmatic decision, and what does everyone believe the right business choice would be. In hindsight, some of the later-stage evolution made it harder to get on mobile, could have made some different choices. In hindsight, if you had just opened it up totally, and been on mobile, that would have been a good choice. There were some technical issues, too.

A lot of it was about competition. The competitive scene for Flash was pretty complicated. Early on, there were a ton of things. Is JavaScript going to make us obsolete? We were pretty sure Java was going to kill us. Then there was VRML—well, "3D must be better." Microsoft was trying their stuff with chrome and direct animation. It was coming from all sides. We were like, okay, let's just focus on making sure this stuff works for our authors, and that we have an integrated solution. That was our focus, more than playing games around openness or not being open.

JM: It's hard to separate the platform from the business environment. Some of the interesting choices there were to make the player, and eventually the compiler, open and free, but selling the authoring environment. Could you talk a bit more about how the plug-in was distributed and how the content and the plug-in were interdependent?

JG: Early on, we didn't set out to own the world by having a player in everyone's browsers. We just thought, we have this tool that creates content, how do we deliver the best content, have the best experience for the customers? So I think not trying to build up leverage helped us. We didn't have our brand out front. It was a key differential with Director.

They were trying to have their brand, and eventually the shock brand. We were like, no, it's all about the developer and their website; we don't need to be in the way. We didn't have a loading logo, all we had was a right-click menu.

Early on, Java, that was going to be a big problem for us. We actually built a version of Flash in Java, but it was kind of slow. Ironically, it kind of worked on the Microsoft browser, [but] we couldn't get it to work on Sun's Java, because it was too slow and buggy. But then Sun sued Microsoft, and got rid of Microsoft's Java, but we just kept building our plug-in.

JM: It seems a differential between Apple and Adobe is who is considered the primary beneficiary? Some would say the end user is Apple's, but that the user interface is king, but you said a goal was to make it as easy to develop for as possible. Do you think there is a balance between user experience and privileging a single distributor, versus making the developer feel as capable as possible and creating a user experience? Flash has been accused of lagging a bit in terms of accessibility, and some of the usability issues early on. Could you talk about that, at the platform level?

JG: Never thought about it too separately. Developer isn't happy if the end user doesn't have a good experience. Getting in people's ways would be trying to show ads in it, or selling behavior information or information about users. We didn't feel as if there were too many hard decisions to make. Everyone was learning about privacy and security early on. Part of the challenge was making it portable. "We don't have a UI," well there wasn't a place to put it. Same thing with accessibility. It's in the operating system. If you put too much in the player, well, we didn't have the engineering resources, but also the player gets too big. Early on, Flash had a remarkable range of capabilities in a platform-independent way but also with a small amount of code. That was a challenging thing. Partly it was just we didn't have the engineers.

JM: So you chose your battles carefully.

JG: Yeah.

JM: Was there anything surprising after or during the project that had to do with the technical implementation, such as the pinball?

JG: That was entirely contrary to what we had in mind, but cool. Some random things, only vaguely related: One thing that was interesting to me from a platform perspective is, early on we did customer visits. There were quite a few architects who were like, thank you, I didn't have a job as an architect, but I can be a Flash designer. It was interesting that someone who had a design sense and wanted to build something that worked, it was an outlet for them. And make money from it. They were running little ten-person design shops building Flash content instead of sweating it out in the basement of an architecture company.

Another random thought, in terms of evolution of the platform. One of the challenging periods in its history from my perspective was when Flash was going like gangbusters with multimedia and advertising and content but the company didn't feel as if there was more revenue to be had. Public company, you have to grow your revenue, well, Enterprise software. Flex was born. I always joked that the original codename for the project was Odyssey. I was like, that's a terrible codename to choose.

There was an internal conflict. We're doing multimedia stuff, how do we make these guys happy versus how do we address the needs of enterprise software developers building front ends for call center applications for whatever, not even just externally facing. We started on externally facing stuff, but once we decided, oh, we want to do internally facing stuff, too, it brought on a whole level of complexity; that's what led to Flex. Flex was a very different model, too, it was a declarative programming language. Which was kind of stylish at the time, people were doing it with XML, but it was a sort of impedance mismatch with the Flash model.

Flash is not what you'd design if you were building that from scratch.

JM: Sort of retrofitting it for enterprise customers, even though that wasn't what it was designed for.

JG: In hindsight, if you look back, it didn't get much traction, hence it got open-sourced. Open source in that sense is, well we're not making much money off of this thing anyway, so there's no chance our competitors will get an edge. That was the netscape strategy, that was also the Flex strategy, but I wasn't a part of that decision. In some sense, if you had better foresight, you would have said, "Well, we should focus on the media," because there was a lot of opportunities just around the corner, mobile, media and gaming.

JM: What are your general thoughts on HTML catching up/adopting things Flash demonstrated first? This is an age-old debate, it seems as if Adobe's impetus is to build up HTML's capabilities so it can continue its focus on tool building. But it seemed to be stymied in debate around the capabilities of CSS/JavaScript in the 2000s. Was this primarily technological or political? Do you think there should always be this trailblazer that has complete control over a reference model that precedes it, or general thoughts on that topic?

JG: I'm sort of a pragmatist. From a technical perspective, I kind of feel HTML is a bit of a train wreck. It's got all of this complexity, and there's not a consistent playback environment. The original promise of

Java, or something like C#, I think it's a crime that there's not a platform like that; good efficient downloadable code with a simple API where people can build lots of stuff on top of it, that's the right answer for the world. The question is, what's the right answer for the companies that influence it? So HTML and CSS is designed for documents and they're good at that, but moving into these other areas, it's a control strategy for these large companies. How do you control the marketplace and manage the change?

My personal opinion is that the open question gets subverted by corporate agendas. It's less a philosophical thing. Step back and look at the situation. What's actually driving the change? What are the benefits for the end users, developers? With our current project, we're mostly focused on building an iOS app, but we also have a web player. Which browser should we support, which video format? Got to test it all. It's a whole bunch of useless costs imposed on this huge community of people. It would have been better if Netscape had won, or something like Java had won. The level of abstraction is terrible. What JavaScript's actually evolved into, the performance of JavaScript, and what you can do with it are amazing.

Sort of related: At some point internally with Flash, I had this idea. Flash in one hundred years. In some sense, Software should be like a book. It's this information that's captured, and the idea that you can actually capture behavior. Since you've been able to capture words and pictures for a long time, what's it mean to capture behavior and have it be part of the human intelligence space? To me it would be nice if there were a simple abstraction that people could build on top of and know it's going to work on their PC or tablet or Google Glass or whatever comes next. It hasn't happened, and HTML certainly isn't it. Java maybe was almost it. Sun had their silly land grab, define as many APIs as I can, I don't care if they work.

JM: You can still run a lot of Flash apps from the early days of Flash. The backward compatibility is pretty good for something that's changed as much. Did you think, can someone run this in ten years?

JG: Well, we certainly didn't have the sense that we'd be that successful early on; we weren't thinking in terms of immortality. We wanted the content to keep working. We felt, as part of being good stewards of the platform, you shouldn't break stuff. Certainly in the early days, what's the life cycle of a website? If I thought about it, I wouldn't know the answer. In some ways, that's the shame of all this. The Internet archive guys: scrape it all and preserve it, but there's so much behavior these days, with back-end servers and things, they are going to be gone.

JM: The whole idea of encapsulating and capturing behavior seems incredibly obvious. Do you think where ActionScript went as a programming language made things more difficult to describe? AS2.0 is still popular, and some are feeling mad at Adobe for removing it?

JG: With the new version of ActionScript, there are two separate issues. With most platform discussions, most people get confused about the difference between API and the programming language. Looking back, I think ActionScript 3 was a little too focused on solving the Flex problem. And the whole ECMAScript thing. We got stranded on a desert isle, well, we thought everyone would go this way, but it turned out the old one was fine, no one wanted to change and the new standard was too complex.

I wish there were a single package or class implementation in JavaScript.

It never should have been JavaScript. I don't know if Java was right, the Java language was fine, but the APIs were terrible. The idea of a virtual machine with JITable code, that seemed like the right idea, and that was the direction we tried to go with ActionScript. Keep the core simple and everything layered on top of it. The entire virtual machine invention keeps it efficient. Nobody has built the right API, and it's hard to get something established. In Java's case, if you want that general platform, you want as simple an API as possible, focus on core abstractions. Turns out if you're IBM or Sun, you want as complicated an API as possible so you can have developers only learn that one, you don't want them to be able to move their code easily.

The right technical solution is subverted by business drivers.

JM: Apple has some heavy lock-ins, but they did open it up to cross-compilers, including Flash eventually. How do you think that went over? Did that open up the walled garden? Was that a win for the developers? It wasn't published as a win for Flash.

JG: It's just a competitive response by Apple. As long as Apple controls the app store. It's amazing that for this dominant platform, it is not actually legal to install software. You bought this iPhone, I should be able to sell software to you. It's got that firewall. It's kind of a crazy situation. The fact that android exists keeps Apple in line to some degree. The app store thing is a disappointment to me as a developer. It should be this open thing, it should be this thing that helps developers make money, but Apple has managed it. From a business perspective, they doesn't really help their developers the way they could to have a profitable ecosystem.

JM: How do you create platforms on top of platforms, such as yours within Apple's ecosystem?

JG: I don't see that as being such a limitation. The thing with the app store was the value people put in it. We did our Kickstarter [project]. We didn't get many comments on it. But one comment was, "Oh, that's too expensive." You spent $600 on a phone, and you're quibbling about this guy trying to charge you $20 for a piece of software. IT's ludicrous. How can you be spending $100 a month on your phone, but you won't spend $2.99? Apple has structured the marketplace. Microsoft, I saw they did a promotion for Windows phone. We'll give you $100 for uploading an app to the app store. I was like, well, $100 doesn't pay for anything. You just want to get a lot of apps and make it feel as if apps should be free and cheap, because there's a ton of free apps. In the early days of Software I was frustrated. You have these shrink-wrapped boxes and these computer stores that are gatekeepers and you have to give them 40 percent and spend so much on marketing and sales. Now, I realize, at least it kept the cost of software up. Now, it's as if software should be free.

JM: I have a labmate writing about free-to-play game lock-in strategies. You have to become more manipulative as a result of the depressed software prices on something like the app store. How as a developer do you justify paying for something when other people are giving it away for free? It was a question early on in Flash works: how do you build a business model around something available for free (the player)?

JG: Certainly with Flash, one of the early frustrations, we charged for the authoring tool and all of the plug-ins were free. We paid Netscape to include the player. If you look at Disney or MSN, who spent millions of dollars building Flash content, Macromedia got a few thousands (or 10,000). Relative to the investment. As opposed to a guy running a development shop who got a much better equation. The monetization strategy is always a problem, and certainly there were people early on trying to charge for players. MPEG-4 guys are probably pissed at Flash, because they wanted to charge per minute and Flash didn't so Flash subverted their strategy to a large degree.

JM: The choice of Apple going with MP4s as their encoding.

JG: The entire MPEG consortium should be illegal. Abuse of the patent system. But because it's twelve companies, it's okay.

JM: Early on, when you saw people creating stand-alone content, did you see people doing things to sell it or otherwise lock it down that weren't necessarily afforded by the initial model? Did that surprise you?

JG: I don't remember any problems or things. Certainly we wanted to enable people. There were some instances of jealousy, where we'd like a piece of the business. Early on we had a product called Generator, which at the time we were afraid, okay, we're not going to get this player out to everyone, how do we take this tool and create something useful? CGI.

We never got much traction, though not long after we gave up on it, there became a market for that sort of thing. But anyway, that's an appealing business, and that was the strategy for Flash video. We're going to make the barriers and costs pretty low. These big companies are spending a lot of money on bandwidth; if we can make their bandwidth cheaper by throttling the flow, they'd be willing to give us a couple percent of their bandwidth costs, because they'd be saving money anyway. We'd have a business where we're getting revenue on the amount of content delivered rather than the number of authors.

JM: Is there anything else in hindsight that if you know how the environment would be, would you make any decisions differently?

JG: The big thing was mobile.

JM: But you guys were tablet PCs in the beginning. You were already ahead of the game.

JG: I remember thinking, if we just had wi-fi at the time pen computers were out. To me that was the key. Having this thing connected to the network where you can make it a content device. The tablet computers we were working on, we were excited because it had a cellular model. It was an analog fax modem. You could fax from the beach. . . . But really, the mobile problem, we saw early on. We spent years trying to work with carriers, read all the articles on how they were investing in new networks for video and multimedia content. My mistake was I believed it. But really it was an excuse to get more spectrum so they could sell more voice minutes, until Apple came along, and because AT&T was in a rough spot, they sold their soul to Apple, and Apple was actually able to deliver a product.

Early on, the first mobile technology, Openwave, had a browser for phones. The idea was, we're not going to put any more memory or processing or better screens on these, so whatever you're going to do, it's going to have to do on hardware for menu options. They had this browser, tag based, you have a list of menu items, and you could click and go to the next menu. It was horrific and slow, and it was going to be the next thing that was to put HTML out of business. But it was so constrained by the operator's constraints that it was a terrible solution. It got on a lot of phones, but nobody ever used it. Kind of like Java on the phone. So Flash was caught in that trap, too. Carriers didn't want to spend hardware on the phones, so what can you do to run in an incredibly constrained environment? So we, Macromedia, build this thing called FlashCast with Flash 1 code ported to a phone, using Flash authoring tool. Made a fair bit of money on it with Docomo, but the carriers weren't motivated to provide a solution related to the business model in any form.

Flash kind of got caught in that. We're trying to build this super light-weight version of the software for the phone, at the same time we're trying to build this enterprise solution that goes the other way. In hindsight, we should have split the difference. We should have had the long-term view that these mobile devices are going to get there, we've just got to be ready. We're not going to let the carriers build something that we knew wasn't going to work well. We need to keep the platform light enough that we could move to this environment. ActionScript 3 should have been simpler, and it should have been this thing that would make sense on a mobile device; you could have obsoleted the old content, but make something that makes sense on a mobile platform. Obviously, the competitive issues of Apple are challenging. But if you had the product, you could have forced Apple's hand to include it.

JM: It was several years after the iPhone was released that touch was integrated into the API.

JG: It wasn't so much the APIs as the performance characteristics for the kind of content. Flash was very lightweight originally. But over time people were developing content for these fast PCs; who cares if it takes 30MB to render this Flash movie, look what it does! Running in a constrained environment, taking advantage of hardware acceleration, Flash didn't map as well as it could have on those platforms.

JM: It grew because computer systems were capable of it. By then, it was hard to go back to when it was that size and take it forward.

JG: We were always constrained because we wanted it to work on older computers, but that's gone now.

JM: It's very hard to achieve the "write once, run anywhere" mandate of Java. It's also hard to get code to adapt to the different uses. How do you think it will look going forward for these different form factors? How will you represent behaviors in the interface, especially with things like wearable interfaces?

JG: It's a question of your abstractions. The interface things. Flash didn't have much of an abstraction, it was pretty low-level [in terms of] what you could do. It was hard to adapt, unless someone wrote a bunch of code to adapt to different screen sizes. HTML originally, if you had flow and resize the window, worked well. This tension between how I'd like it to look good on one device versus how I want it to have a model and structure that'd work well on a bunch of different devices. Classic engineering problem. No magic answer. We're struggling now. Everybody says you have to build a separate UI for phone and tablets. That's kind of expensive.

JM: Flex came pretty close to a device-independent GUI kit, based on Touch or WIMP. It was pretty impressive. Good solutions don't always work out in the marketplace.

JG: It's tough to get the right level on those abstractions. Artists want to have a lot of flexibility, having this structure that knows how to adapt itself. With iPhone apps, everyone wants to reskin it so they can make it their own.

JM: Where's the Internet in ten years? Best, worst, pragmatic?

JG: Kind of too big a question. Vision with our current project, here's an incredibly fluid experience. Capture it and add your editorial on top of it. You can't just lean back. It's like writing a book. I had this joke: if you were cavemen, and you happened to have an iPhone, and you didn't know how to read or write, how would you capture information? Obviously writing and reading information on these things is kind of painful. What's this tool you can use for capturing an experience of the world? Not just for capturing, but for learning, how to build a car or garden or farm. It's amazing how terrible we are as a culture at capturing some of these forms of information. Making cheese, there's no book you can buy on making cheese. There's a guy over there who knows how to make cheese, and he didn't teach it to somebody else, it's gone. New models of information and communication are interesting. The negative side, it's crazy that somebody knows where I am at any point of the day and read all my emails and knows who I knows and targets me. For credit cards, where they say, we think somebody has your number, let's send a new number.

That device there. You realize there's no security dialogue you had to activate to record our conversation. It's a bit of an oversight. Any application you decided to download, you could put in a bit of processing.

JM: You can sneak it past the app police.

JG: They have no ability to test that stuff. That testing is an illusion. The idea that Apple can claim they'd get security through their QA is just ridiculous.

JG: [On future] With Flash, we had lot of exciting stuff. We wake up in the morning, what's the Shock site of the day, was it Flash or Director? Oh, it's Flash, look at what they did; how'd they do that? Look at this community, doing the Flash film festival, and conferences where people were excited doing this stuff.

Well, Flash video, what's the number one issue with that?

Well, probably porn, and a lot of Asian girls sitting in front of a webcam streaming through the Flash media server, and corporate advertising trying to influence people's behavior.

JM: It feels as if it's grown up and done some things. Especially Elit—removing the gatekeepers. You have to create a CD-ROM and print it. We've been looking at these communities. Apple still has content filtering.

JG: Microsoft had a product called Direct Animation. A funny industry story. In terms of competitive platforms, Microsoft had this platform, and they were one of our big partners for distributing the player, because they included it with Windows. Well, we're doing this platform, we'd rather you get rid of your player and just build stuff on our player. Have your authoring tool and compete with all the other authoring tools on a level playing field. We were a little guy, we don't know what to do, so we had a project to take our authoring tool and target their platform. And we did a demo, kind of a skunkworks project. We went out and did a big demo. We worked hard on this thing, and look what it does, and it was terrible. Because their platform was terrible. It was some mathematicians doing a multimedia platform, right, and they were like, I have this great idea for how to describe the formulas of animation. It's in the designer's head, it's not in a mathematical formula. It was slow, and it was a funny moment because when we got out of the meeting, one of the product managers said, "I've never been rolled so well before." It wasn't intentional, but we totally ambushed them in front of their bosses.

JM: By showing them how bad their platform is?

JG: Yeah, they were about to get renewed for their next round of funding, but they were like, wait, it doesn't work? Not that we did it, we didn't make the platform bad, but it never saw the light of day after that.

JM: What about the very first tween? You were talking about continuous versus discrete.

JG: So the originally tweening in Flash was sort of, well, make an easy way to do the tweens, have the computer do some of the work. If you look at the new style, it's trying to be more like the property-based animation. Part of the issue for Flash is that it didn't give really good control over individual properties of an object, such as acceleration and deceleration, because of the model we used. Which made it good for interactive things, and for things moving on and off the screen, but it wasn't so good for motion graphics.

JM: [Talking about conception, timeline staying through it, and how we conceptualize motion in our head] Do you think that speaks to how we conceptualize motion in our head?

JG: Back to the coding by example. It's one thing to sort of play around, get it right, then I'll just sort of add behavior. Some of the more mathematically based animation tools, you really have to think ahead: what is the structure underneath this, what do I want to achieve, okay, I'm going to set up my objects one way, my hierarchy, my properties and variables, There's much more planning. Obviously there's stuff to plan with the Flash model as well, but you have a little more choice.

JM: More quick and iterative.

JG: And it's funny, too, developing an iOS app. I built this product, IntelliDraw, one of the first commercial constraint-based drawing packages. So I should understand constraints. Apple now got their constraint-based UI, came in iOS version 6, pushing it harder in iOS version 7. They have a much more sophisticated model.

Works Cited

ActionSick, DawnOfDusk, KevnSevn, Knyszekanimated, NYSKA, and Zrb. 2008. "The Super Platformer Tutorial Collab '08." Newgrounds. August 20. Accessed June 5, 2013. http:///www.newgrounds.com/portal/view/455972.

Adobe. 2008. SWF File Format Specification Version 10. Adobe Systems Incorporated. Accessed June 10, 2013. http://www.adobe.com/devnet/swf.html.

Adobe. 2012. "Flash Player Developer Center." Adobe Developer Connection. Accessed January 5, 2013. http://www.adobe.com/devnet/flashplayer.html.

Adobe. 2013. "Adobe Premium Features for the Flash Player." January. Accessed August 20, 2013. http://www.adobe.com/devnet/flashplayer/articles/premium -features.html.

Allbusiness.com. 1996. "MSN Goes Online with FutureSplash Animator." December 10. Accessed March 6, 2014. http://web.archive.org/web/20100107023410/http:// www.allbusiness.com/technology/software-services-applications-internet/ 7295780-1.html.

Animation World Network. 1999. "Goddamn George Liquor Program." Annie Awards. http://www.awn.com/annieawards/george.php3. Accessed January 5, 2012.

Apple. 2007. "Apple Reinvents the Phone with iPhone." January 9. Press Info. http:// www.apple.com/pr/library/2007/01/09Apple-Reinvents-the-Phone-with -iPhone.html. Accessed December 6, 2012.

Apple. 2010. "Apple Launches iPad." Press Info. January 27. Accessed July 6, 2013. http://www.apple.com/pr/library/2010/01/27Apple-Launches-iPad.html.

Apple. 2013. "App Review." Accessed August 22, 2013. https://developer.apple.com/ appstore/guidelines.html.

Armor Games. 2008. "Achievement Unlocked." Newgrounds. December 18. Accessed July 11, 2013. http://www.newgrounds.com/portal/view/474371.

Armstrong, Josh. 2007. "Phil Nibbelink: Sealed with a Kiss." Animated Views. Accessed May 18, 2013. http://animatedviews.com/2007/phil-nibbelink-sealed -with-a-kiss.

Arthegall. 2012. "Jonathan Gay Interview." March 20. Accessed March 6, 2014. http://
macintoshgarden.org/forum/jonathan-gay-interview.

Bardzell, J. 2005. "Creativity in Amateur Multimedia: Popular Culture, Critical Theory,
and HCI." *Human Technology: An Interdisciplinary Journal on Humans in ICT Environments* 3 (1): 12–33.

Benmergui, Daniel. 2008. *I wish I were the Moon*. September 26. Accessed October 5,
2012. http://www.kongregate.com/games/danielben/i-wish-i-were-the-moon.

Berners-Lee, Tim. 1994. "The World-Wide Web." *Communications of the ACM* 37 (8):
76–82.

Bogost, Ian. 2007. *Persuasive Games*. Cambridge, MA: MIT Press.

Bogost, Ian. 2010. "Cow Clicker: The Making of Obsession". July 21. Accessed August
20, 2013. http://www.bogost.com/blog/cow_clicker_1.shtml.

Bogost, Ian. 2011a. "Shit Crayons." March 3. Accessed June 5, 2012. http://www
.bogost.com/writing/shit_crayons.shtml.

Bogost, Ian. 2011b. *How to Do Things with Videogames*. Minneapolis, MN: University of
Minnesota Press.

Bogost, Ian. 2013. "OAUTH OF FEALTY: Resignation beyond Sorrow on the Facebook
Platform and Beyond." August 1. Accessed August 20, 2013. http://www.bogost
.com/blog/oauth_of_fealty.shtml.

Bogost, Ian, Simon Ferrari, and Bobby Schweizer. 2010. *Newsgames: Journalism at
Play*. Cambridge, MA: MIT Press.

Bollier, David. 2008. *Viral Spiral: How the Commoners Built a Digital Republic of Their
Own*. New York: The New Press.

Bouhlel, Yassine. 2010. "A Nostalgic Rummage through the History of Flash." Active
Tuts Plus. December 31. Accessed October 16, 2012. http://code.tutsplus.com/
articles/a-nostalgic-rummage-through-the-history-of-flash--active-6733.

Brown, Janelle. 1997. "Bugs Bunny, Meet Bozlo Beaver." *Wired*. November 4. Accessed
February 5, 2012. http://www.wired.com/culture/lifestyle/news/1997/11/8243.

Cannasse, Nicolas. 2012. "Adobe Announces Speed Tax." March 28. Accessed March
30, 2012. http://ncannasse.fr/blog/adobe_announce_speed_tax.

Canter, Marc. 2003. "The Birth of MacroMind." August. Accessed November 2, 2013.
https://web.archive.org/web/20040203015311/http:/blogs.it/0100198/
stories/2003/06/12/theNewParadigmOfTools.html.

Carter, Ashley. 2004. "Lil' Pimp: Directed by Peter Gilstrap and Mark Brooks."
Exclaim. December. Accessed January 4, 2012. http://exclaim.ca/Reviews/Dvd/
lil_pimp-peter_gilstrap_mark_brooks.

Chambers, Mike. 2011. "Clarifications on Flash Player for Mobile Browsers, the Flash
Platform, and the Future of Flash." November 11. Accessed August 6, 2013. http://
www.mikechambers.com/blog/2011/11/11/clarifications-on-flash-player-for
-mobile-browsers-the-flash-platform-and-the-future-of-flash.

Charles, Alec. 2009. "Playing with One's Self: Notions of Subjectivity and Agency in
Digital Games." *Eludamos: Journal for Computer Game Culture* 3 (2): 281–294.

Cramer, Florian. 2008. "Language." In *Software Studies: A Lexicon*, ed. Matthew Fuller,
168–173. Cambridge, MA: MIT Press.

Create JS. 2013. "EaselJS." May. Accessed August 2, 2013. http://www.createjs.com/#!/
EaselJS.

Croteau, John. 1999. "Score Tutorial." Flash Bible. Accessed March 19, 2012. http://
www.flashbible.com.

Cummings, Alastair H. 2007. "The Evolution of Game Controllers and Control Schemes and Their Effect on Their Games." *Multimedia Systems Conference*. Accessed February 5, 2013. http://mms.ecs.soton.ac.uk/2007/papers/6.pdf.

Curtis, Hillman. 2002. "Introduction." In *WWW Design: Flash—The Best Web Sites from Around the World*, ed. Daniel Donnelly, 6–7. Gloucester, MA: Rockport Publishers.

Daubs, M. S. 2006. "Flashimation: The Context and Culture of Web Animation." Siggraph.org. Accessed June 10, 2013. http://www.siggraph.org/artdesign/gallery/S06/paper1.pdf.

David, Matthew. 2003. "What's New in Flash MX 2004?" *InformIT*. October 24. Accessed July 3, 2013. http://www.informit.com/articles/article.aspx?p=101632.

Doull, David. 2001. "Building Games in Flash." Flash Kit. Accessed May 12, 2013. http://www.flashkit.com/tutorials/Games/Building-David_Do-598/index.php.

Dugan, Lauren. 2011. "Updates to TweetDeck Get Rid of Adobe Air for HTML5, Ditch All Networks Other than Twitter And Facebook." December 9. Accessed December 11, 2013. https://www.mediabistro.com/alltwitter/updates-to-tweetdeck-get-rid-of-adobe-air-for-html5-ditch-all-networks-other-than-twitter-and-facebook_b16632.

Edge Staff. 2007. "Flash of Genius." *Edge Magazine*. July 6. Accessed July 23, 2013. http://www.edge-online.com/features/feature-flash-genius.

Eisler, Craig. 2012. "Starting February 1, 2012: Use the Power of Kinect for Windows to Change the World." MSDN. January 9. Accessed November 6, 2012. http://blogs.msdn.com/b/kinectforwindows/archive/2012/01/09/kinect-for-windows-commercial-program-announced.aspx.

Elliott, Jake. 2010. *I Can Hold My Breath Forever*. March 30. Accessed June 5, 2013. http://dai5ychain.net/breath.

Falcon, Alvaris. 2013. "HTML5 Website Showcase: 48 Potential Flash-Killing Demos." August 28. Accessed September 5, 2013. http://www.hongkiat.com/blog/48-excellent-html5-demos.

FlashForward. 2004. "11th Flashforward Conference Tops 15,000 Total Attendance." *DesignTaxi*. February 1. Accessed July 9, 2013. http://designtaxi.com/news/157/11th-Flashforward-Conference-tops-15-000-total-attendance.

Flash Kit. 2001. *Flash Kit Tutorials & Articles*. February 7. Accessed July 6, 2013. http://web.archive.org/web/20010207042615/http://www.flashkit.com/tutorials/Interactivity/more3.shtml.

Flores, Leonardo. 2013. "Liberating Flash: The Case of Remixwork and Dreaming Methods." *MLA 2014 Panel: Literature after Flash*. May 31. Accessed August 10, 2013. http://www.scribd.com/doc/144951780/Liberating-Flash-The-Case-of-Remixworx-and-Dreaming-Methods.

Forshaw, James. 2011. "WebGL—A New Dimension for Browser Exploitation." May 9. Accessed February 5, 2013. http://www.contextis.com/research/blog/webgl-new-dimension-browser-exploitation.

Frank, Jenn. 2012. "A Conversation with Game Developer Jake Elliott." February 10. Accessed November 10, 2013. http://www.unwinnable.com/2012/02/10/a-conversation-with-jake-elliott/#.Uo5PCMRDs2c.

Frasca, Gonzalo. 2003. *September 12th*. Accessed October 5, 2013. http://www.newsgaming.com/games/index12.htm.

Free Software Foundation. 2013. "The Free Software Definition." June 18. Accessed November 22, 2013. http://www.gnu.org/philosophy/free-sw.html.

Fuller, Matthew. 2006. "Introduction." In *Software Studies: A Lexicon*, ed. Matthew Fuller, 1–14. Cambridge, MA: MIT Press.

Fulp, Tom. 1999. "Pico's School." Newgrounds. April 30. Accessed December 3, 2012. http://www.newgrounds.com/portal/view/310349.

Fulp, Tom. 2013a. "Flash Portal History: 2000." Newgrounds. Accessed March 6, 2013. http://www.newgrounds.com/collection/flashportalhistory2000.

Fulp, Tom. 2013b. "Flash Portal History: 2002." Newgrounds. Accessed November 20, 2013. http://www.newgrounds.com/collection/flashportalhistory2002.

Fulton, Jeff, and Steve Fulton. 2010. *The Essential Guide to Flash Games*. New York: Apress.

Galbraith, Patrick W. 2011. "Bishōjo Games: 'Techno-Intimacy' and the Virtually Human in Japan." *Game Studies* 11 (12). May. Accessed November 5, 2012. http://gamestudies.org/1102/articles/galbraith.

Gambit. 2010. *Elude*. May 20. Accessed July 3, 2013. http://gambit.mit.edu/loadgame/elude.php.

Gaudrealt, Geoffrey P. 2004. *Sploder!* Accessed July 20, 2013. http://www.sploder.com.

Gay, Jonathan. 1996. "Shape Technology." Accessed June 10, 2012. http://web.archive.org/web/19961105023524/http://www.futurewave.com/shapetechnology.htm.

Georgenes, Chris. 2014. *How to Cheat in Adobe Flash CC*. Burlington, MA: Focal Press.

Gilmore, John. 2005. *[Gnash] Welcome to the Gnash Project!* December 20. Accessed June 10, 2012. http://archive.is/WFsx.

Goldstone, Will. 2013. "Native 2D Tools." *Unity Company Blog*. August 28. Accessed November 22, 2013. http://blogs.unity3d.com/2013/08/28/unity-native-2d-tools.

Goss, Emma. 2013. "Sorry Steve Jobs, Someone Else Thought of the iPhone First." Huffington Post. August 13. Accessed August 25, 2013. http://www.huffington-post.com/emma-goss/sorry-steve-jobs-someone-_b_3748404.html.

Green, Joshua, and Henry Jenkins. 2011. "Spreadable Media: How Audiences Create Value and Meaning in a Networked Economy." In *The Handbook of Media Audiences*, ed. Virginia Nightingale, 109–127. New York: Wiley-Blackwell.

Grigar, Dene, and Stuart Moulthrop. 2013. "Pathfinders." May 21. Accessed August 15, 2013. http://dtc-wsuv.org/wp/pathfinders.

Grossman, Lev. 2006. "You—Yes, You—Are TIME's Person of the Year." *TIME Magazine*. December 25. Accessed July 22, 2013. http://www.time.com/time/magazine/article/0,9171,1570810,00.html.

Hague, Jim Ver, and Chris Jackson. 2006. *Flash 3D: Animation, Interactivity, and Games*. Burlington, MA: Focal Press.

Haxe. 2013. *HaXe*. August 20. Accessed August 20, 2013. http://haxe.org.

Hayles, N. Katherine. 2002. "ELMCIP." *Deeper into the Machine: The Future of Electronic Literature*. April 6. Accessed June 1, 2013. http://elmcip.net/critical-writing/deeper-machine-future-electronic-literature.

Hayles, N. Katherine. 2007. "Electronic Literature: What Is It?" *Electronic Literature Organization*. January 2. Accessed June 15, 2013. http://eliterature.org/pad/elp.html.

Hayles, N. Katherine, Nick Montfort, Scott Rettberg, and Stephanie Strickland. 2006. *Electronic Literature Collection*. October. Accessed July 1, 2013. http://collection. eliterature.org/1/aux/about.html.

Heid, Jim. 2000. "Flash 5." *MacWorld*. December 9. Accessed October 5, 2013. http:// www.macworld.com/article/1015848/flash.html.

Helgason, David. 2013. *Sunsetting Flash*. April 23. Accessed May 5, 2013. http://blogs .unity3d.com/2013/04/23/sunsetting-flash.

Hinkle, David. 2012. "Alien Hominid Has Been Played 20 Million Times on New-grounds." *Joystiq*. May 9. Accessed June 3, 2013. http://www.joystiq .com/2012/05/09/alien-hominid-has-been-played-20-million-times-on -newgrounds.

Hollis, Line. 2009. *Daniel Benmergui and the Gulf of Execution*. July 12. Accessed November 21, 2013. http://www.linehollis.com/2009/07/12/daniel-benmergui -and-the-gulf-of-execution.

Homestar Runner. 2006. *Everything Else, V. 2*. DVD.

Internet Archive. 2012. *80 Terabytes of Archived Web Crawl Data Available for Research*. October 26. Accessed July 5, 2013. http://blog.archive.org/2012/10/26/80 -terabytes-of-archived-web-crawl-data-available-for-research.

Jana, Reena, and Mark Tribe. 2006. *New Media Art*. New York: Taschen.

Jenkins, Henry. 1992. *Textual Poachers: Television Fans and Participatory Culture*. New York: Routledge.

Jenkins, Henry. 2006. *Fans, Bloggers, and Gamers: Exploring Participatory Culture*. New York: NYU Press.

Jobs, Steve. 2010. "Thoughts on Flash." *Apple.com*. April. Accessed August 5, 2013. http://www.apple.com/hotnews/thoughts-on-flash.

Jones, Steven Edward, and George Kuriakose Thiruvathukal. 2012. *Codename Revolution: The Nintendo Wii Platform*. Cambridge, MA: MIT Press.

Juul, Jesper. 2010. *A Casual Revolution: Reinventing Video Games and Their Players*. Cambridge, MA: MIT Press.

Kayali, Fares, and Josef Schuh. 2011. "Retro Evolved: Level Design Practice Exempli-fied by the Contemporary Retro Game." *DiGRA Proceedings 2011: Think Design Play*. September 17. Accessed July 13, 2013. http://www.digra.org/wp-content/uploads/ digital-library/11313.03271.pdf.

Kincaid, Jason. 2009. "Heyzap Brings Xbox Live-Style Achievements to Flash Gaming." *TechCrunch*. December 1. Accessed July 5, 2013. http://techcrunch.com/2009/ 12/01/heyzap-flash-achievement.

Kricfalusi, John. 2012. "John K's 'Cans without Labels.'" Kickstarter. July 17. Accessed November 23, 2012. http://www.kickstarter.com/projects/1056985656/john-ks -cans-without-labels.

Kristin. 2004. "Is the Flash Community Dead?" *GalaxyGoo Blogs*. August 27. Accessed July 5, 2013. http://www.galaxygoo.org/blogs/2004/08/is_the_flash_community _dead.html.

Krzywinska, Tanya. 2012. "The Strange Case of the Misappearance of Sex in Video Games." In *Computer Games and New Media Cultures: A Handbook of Digital Game Studies*, ed. Johannes Fromme and Alexander Unger, 143–160. New York: Springer.

Kumparak, Greg. 2013. "Flash Takes Another Step towards Death as Unity Drops Support." *Tech Crunch*. April 24. Accessed May 5, 2013. http://techcrunch

.com/2013/04/24/flash-takes-another-step-towards-death-as-unity-drops
-support.

Leishman, Donna. 2012. "The Flash Community: Implications for Post-Conceptual-
ism." *Dichtun Digital*. Accessed May 5, 2013. http://www.dichtung-digital
.org/2012/41/leishman/leishman.htm.

Lessig, Lawrence. 2008. *Remix: Making Art and Commerce Thrive in the Hybrid Economy*.
New York: Penguin.

Lewis, Chris, Noah Wardrip-Fruin, and Jim Whitehead. 2012. "Motivational Game
Design Patterns of 'Ville Games." In *Proceedings of the International Conference on
the Foundations of Digital Games '12*, 172–179. New York: ACM Press.

Liszkiewicz, A. J. Patrick. 2010. "Cultivated Play: Farmville." *Berfrois*. October 21.
Accessed November 12, 2013. http://www.berfrois.com/2010/10/cultivated
-play-farmville.

MacManus, Richard. 2004. "Interview with Marc Canter." readwrite. March 29.
http://readwrite.com/2004/03/29/interview_with#awesm=~onsZyqO16L1IuX
(accessed November 4, 2013).

Macromedia, Inc. 1997. "Macromedia Director and Flash to Deliver Java-Based Multimedia." *The Free Website*. October 7. Accessed August 20, 2013. http://www
.thefreelibrary.com/Macromedia+Director+and+Flash+to+Deliver+Java
-Based+Multimedia-a019831587.

Macromedia, Inc. 2002. *Macromedia Flash MX Application Development Center*. Accessed
July 1, 2013. http://web.archive.org/web/20020905105907/http:/www.macro
media.com/desdev/mx/flash.

Maher, Jimmy. 2012. *The Future Was Here: The Commodore Amiga*. Cambridge, MA: MIT
Press.

Manovich, Lev. 2001. *The Language of New Media*. Cambridge, MA: MIT Press.

Manovich, Lev. 2005. "Generation Flash." In *Total Interaction*, ed. Gerhard M.
Buurman, 66–77. New York: Springer.

Manovich, Lev. 2013. *Software Takes Command*. New York: Bloomsbury.

Marino, Mark C. 2006. "Critical Code Studies." *Electronic Book Review*. December 4.
Accessed June 9, 2013. http://electronicbookreview.com/thread/electropoetics/
codology.

Martinelli, Nicole. 2009. "Q & A: How Sex Game Apps Get Approved By Apple." Cult
of Mac. July 16. Accessed October 20, 2012. http://www.cultofmac.com/13082/q
-a-how-sex-game-apps-get-approved-by-apple.

McEntee, Jonathan, and Edmund McMillen. 2008. "Meat Boy." Newgrounds.
October 5. Accessed June 7, 2013. http://www.newgrounds.com/portal/view/
463241.

McLuhan, Marshall. 1964. *Understanding Media: The Extensions of Man*. Cambridge,
MA: MIT Press.

Millward Brown. 2009. "Flash Player Penetration." *Adobe Flash*. February. Accessed
January 3, 2013. http://photos.pcpro.co.uk/blogs/wp-content/uploads/2009/02/
blogflashplayerstats.jpg.

Molleindustria. 2011. *Phone Story*. September 9. Accessed April 16, 2013. http://www
.phonestory.org.

Montfort, Nick, Patsy Baudoin, John Bell, Ian Bogost, Jeremy Douglass, Mark C.
Marino, Michael Mateas, Casey Reas, Mark Sample, and Noah Vawter. 2012. *10
PRINT CHR$(205.5+RND(1)); GOTO 10*. Cambridge, MA: MIT Press.

Montfort, Nick, and Ian Bogost. 2009. *Racing the Beam: The Atari Video Computer System*. Cambridge, MA: MIT Press.

Moock, Colin. 2001. *ActionScript: The Definitive Guide—Mastering Flash Programming*. New York: O'Reilly Media.

Moulthrop, Stuart. 2008. "Pax, Writing, and Change." *Electronic Book Review*. February 29. Accessed June 15, 2013. http://www.electronicbookreview.com/thread/firstperson/terminal.

Moulthrop, Stuart. 2013. E-mail message to author. July 15, 2013.

Mulcahy, Stacey. 2006. "Flash: Ten Years, Ten Perspectives." *Flash Tenth Anniversary*. Accessed July 23, 2013. http://solutionpartners.adobe.com/designcenter/dialogbox/flash_anniversary/index_09.html.

Murray, John. 2012. Interview with Arno Gourdol. February 3, 2012.

Nelson, Jason. 2007. *Game, Game, Game and Again Game*. Accessed July 10, 2013. http://www.secrettechnology.com/gamegame/gamegame.html.

Newgrounds. n.d. "Art Games." Newgrounds. Accessed July 5, 2013. http://www.newgrounds.com/collection/artgames.

Newsgrounds. 2008. "Newgrounds Achievement Api." Newgrounds. May 4. Accessed July 11, 2013. http://www.newgrounds.com/bbs/topic/932923.

New York Times. 2001. "Report Counts Computers in Majority of U.S. Homes." *New York Times*. September 7: http://www.nytimes.com/2001/09/07/us/report-counts-computers-in-majority-of-us-homes.html.

Nielsen, Jakob. 2000. "Flash: 99% Bad." Jakob Nielsen's Alertbox. October 29. Accessed November 17, 2012. http://www.nngroup.com/articles/flash-99-percent-bad.

Norman, Donald A. 1988. *The Psychology of Everyday Things*. New York: Basic Books.

Nutt, Christian. 2013. "Nintendo's Indies Guy Tells You How to Get Your Games Approved." *Gamasutra*. March 25. Accessed August 1, 2013. http://www.gamasutra.com/view/news/189180/Nintendos_Adelman_talks_easier_requirements_for_3DS_Wii_U_indie_dev.php.

Obadike, Keith, and Mendi Obadike. 2006. "The Black.net.art Actions." In *Re: Skin*, ed. Mary Flanagan and Austin Booth, 245–250. Cambridge, MA: MIT Press.

Occupy Flash. 2013. Occupy Flash. Accessed August 10, 2013. http://www.occupyflash.org.

Parr, Ben. 2011. "Adobe Admits: Apple Won, Flash for Mobile Is Done, HTML5 Is the Future." *Mashable*. November 11. Accessed March 6, 2014. http://mashable.com/2011/11/11/flash-mobile-dead-adobe.

Parrott, Dominic J., and Amos Zeichner. 2003. "Effects of Hypermasculinity on Physical Aggression against Women." *Psychology of Men & Masculinity* 4 (1): 70.

Peters, Keith, Manny Tan, Jamie MacDonald, et al. 2004. *Flash Math Creativity*, 2nd ed. Berkeley, CA: Friends of ED.

Piilonen, Eli, Luka Marcetic, and David Carney. 2009. "The Company of Myself." Newgrounds. November 22. Accessed July 2, 2013. http://www.newgrounds.com/portal/view/518729.

Pressman, Jessica. 2009. "Pacific Rim Digital Modernism: The Electronic Literature of Young-Hae Chang Heavy Industries." In *Pacific Rim Modernisms*, ed. Steve Yao, Mary Ann Gillies, and Helen Sword, 316–334. Toronto: University of Toronto Press.

Raymond, Eric S. 1999. *The Cathedral and the Bazaar*. Sebastopol, CA: O'Reilly Media.

Rehak, Bob. 2003. "Playing at Being: Psychoanalysis and the Avatar." In *The Video Game Theory Reader*, ed. Mark J. P. Wolf and Bernard Perron, 103–128. New York: Routledge.

Rettberg, Scott. 2010. "Disasters Natural and Digital: The Secret Technologies of Jason Nelson." *ELMCIP*. Accessed July 10, 2013. http://elmcip.net/critical-writing/disasters-natural-and-digital-secret-technologies-jason-nelson.

Reynolds, Ben. 2011. *Sidescrolling Platformer ~Part 1~ Setup and Planning*. November 11. Accessed July 5, 2013. http://as3gametuts.com/2011/11/11/platformer-1.

Rockwell, Geoffrey M., and Kevin Kee. 2011. "The Leisure of Serious Games: A Dialogue." *Game Studies* 11 (2). May. Accessed May 5, 2013. http://gamestudies .org/1102/articles/geoffrey_rockwell_kevin_kee.

Rosenblatt, Seth. 2013. "Google Chrome Browser Turns 5." *CNET*. September 2. Accessed September 2, 2013. http://www.cbsnews.com/8301-205_162 -57600963/google-chrome-browser-turns-5.

Rusch, Doris Carmen. 2010. "The Art of Nailing Pudding to the Wall—Strategies on Modeling Abstract Concepts in Games." *Meaningful Play Proceedings*. October 23. Accessed July 12, 2013. http://meaningfulplay.msu.edu/proceedings2010/ mp2010_paper_24.pdf.

Saltsman, Adam. 2011. "EZPlatfomer Tutorial." *Flash Game Dojo*. January 28. Accessed July 5, 2013. http://flashgamedojo.com/wiki/index.php?title=EZPlatformer_%2 8Flixel%29.

Sample, Mark. 2013. "Electronic Literature after Flash (MLA 14 Proposal)." *Sample Reality*. April 10. Accessed August 20, 2013. http://www.samplereality .com/2013/04/10/electronic-literature-after-flash-mla14-proposal.

Scharrer, Erica. 2004. "Virtual Violence: Gender and Aggression in Video Game Advertisements." *Mass Communication and Society* 7 (4): 353–376.

Selepak, Andrew. 2010. "Skinhead Super Mario Brothers: An Examination of Racist and Violent Games on White Supremacist Web Sites." *Journal of Criminal Justice and Popular Culture* 17 (1): 1–47.

Shankland, Stephen. 2012. "Adobe Touts Tools for Flash-to-HTML Conversion." *CNET*. April 3. Accessed August 8, 2013. http://news.cnet.com/8301-30685_3 -57407926-264/adobe-touts-tools-for-flash-to-html-conversion.

Shirky, Clay. 2011. *Cognitive Surplus: How Technology Makes Consumers into Collaborators*. New York: Penguin.

SilverStitch. 2013. *Silver Stitch on Deviant Art*. June 15. Accessed July 10, 2013. http:// silver-stitch.deviantart.com.

sim-man. 2002. "SIMGIRLS Version 5.1." Newgrounds. April 18. Accessed November 6, 2013. www.newgrounds.com/portal/view/50364.

Simpson, Aaron. 2006. "The Flash Animation 10—Most Influential." *Cold Hard Flash*. September 21. Accessed March 6, 2013. http://www.coldhardflash.com/2006/09/ flash-animation-10.html.

Simpson, Aaron. 2007. "John K's Guide to Surviving the End of Television." *Cold Hard Flash*. April 23. Accessed March 7, 2013. http://www.coldhardflash.com/2007/04/ john-ks-guide-to-surviving-end-of.html.

Simpson, Aaron. 2008. "Grandmasters of Flash: An Interview with the Creators of Flash." *Cold Hard Flash*. February 12. Accessed June 5, 2013. http://www .coldhardflash.com/2008/02/grandmasters-of-flash-an-interview-with-the -creators-of-flash.html.

Sinclair, Carla. 1999. "That's Not All, Folks." *The Industry Standard*. October 25. Accessed August 12, 2013. http://web.archive.org/web/20020202164951/www .thestandard.com/article/0,1902,6967,00.html.

Smith, Aaron. 2013. *Smartphone Ownership 2013*. June 5. Accessed August 10, 2013. http://www.pewinternet.org/Reports/2013/Smartphone-Ownership-2013/ Findings.aspx.

Sploder. 2004. "About Sploder™." Accessed July 9, 2013. http://www.sploder.com/ about.php.

Stone, Brad. 2010. *Google's Andy Rubin on Everything Android*. April 27. Accessed July 10, 2013. http://bits.blogs.nytimes.com/2010/04/27/googles-andy-rubin-on -everything-android.

Stoneback, Robert. 2009. "Apple's Forbidden Fruit." *The Escapist*. September 15. Accessed December 9, 2012. http://www.escapistmagazine.com/articles/view/ issues/issue_219/6518-Apples-Forbidden-Fruit.

Stuart, Keith. 2011. "Basquiat Meets Mario Brothers? Digital Poet Jason Nelson on the Meaning of Art Games." *The Guardian*. September 13. Accessed June 12, 2013. http://www.guardian.com/technology/gamesblog/2011/sep/13/the -meaning-of-art-games.

Sturman, David. 1998. "Retrospective: The State of Computer Animation." *ACM SIG- GRAPH1* 32 (1): 57–61.

Sullivan, Jennifer. 1997. "In His Way, John K. Will Challenge the World." *Wired*. October 8. Accessed September 5, 2012. http://www.wired.com/culture/lifestyle/ news/1997/10/7566.

Suominen, Jaakko. 2008. "The Past as the Future? Nostalgia and Retrogaming in Digital Culture." *Fibreculture 11*. November 1. Accessed July 13, 2013. http://www .journal.fibreculture.org/issue11/issue11_suominen_print.html.

Tearse, Brandon, Peter Mawhorter, Michael Mateas, and Noah Wardrip-Fruin. 2012. "Lessons Learned From a Rational Radical Reconstruction of Minstrel." *Proceedings of the Twenty-Sixteen AAAI Conference on Artificial Intelligence*. July 26. Accessed July 13, 2013. https://games.soe.ucsc.edu/lessons-learned-rational -reconstruction-minstrel.

Tim W. 2008. "Interview: Daniel Benmergui (I Wish I Were the Moon)." December 10. Accessed July 7, 2013. http://www.indiegames.com/2008/12/interview _daniel_benmergui_i_w.html.

Tribe, Mark. 2007a. "Mendi and Keith Obadike." *New Media Art*. February 15. Accessed June 29, 2013. https://wiki.brown.edu/confluence/display/MarkTribe/Mendi +and+Keith+Obadike.

Tribe, Mark. 2007b. "Young-Hae Chang Heavy Industries." *New Media Art*. February 22. Accessed July 9, 2013. https://wiki.brown.edu/confluence/display/ MarkTribe/Young-Hae+Chang+Heavy+Industries.

Tyler, Tom. 2008. "A Procrustean Probe." *Game Studies* 8 (2). December. Accessed February 5, 2013. http://gamestudies.org/0802/articles/tyler.

Tynes, John. 2008. "Prismatic Play: Games as Windows on the Real World." *Electronic Book Review*. March 26. Accessed July 5, 2013. http://www.electronicbookreview .com/thread/firstperson/relevant.

Vaughan-Nichols, Steven J. 2011. "Flash Is Dead. Long Live HTML5." *2DNet*. November 9. Accessed July 12, 2013. http://www.zdnet.com/blog/networking/ flash-is-dead-long-live-html5/1633.

Veale, Kevin. 2012. "'Interactive Cinema' Is an Oxymoron, but May Not Always Be." *Game Studies* 12 (1). September. Accessed December 2, 2012. http://gamestudies .org/1201/articles/veale.

Voerman, Matt. 2006. "Flash: Ten Years, Ten Perspectives." *Flash Tenth Anniversary*. Accessed July 12, 2013. http://solutionpartners.adobe.com/designcenter/ dialogbox/flash_anniversary/index_04.html.

W3C. 2012. *HTML5 Definition Complete, W3C Moves to Interoperability Testing and Performance*. December 17. Accessed May 5, 2013. http://www.w3.org/2012/12/html5 -cr.html.en.

W3C. 2013. *HTML Canvas 2D Context*. August 6. Accessed August 16, 2013. http://www .w3.org/TR/2dcontext.

Wardrip-Fruin, Noah. 2009. *Expressive Processing*. Cambridge, MA: MIT Press.

Warren, Jonathan, Sharon Stoerger, and Ken Kelley. 2011. "Longitudinal Gender and Age Bias in a Prominent Amateur New Media Community. *New Media & Society* 14 (1): 7–27.

We Create Stuff. 2007. *Portal: The Flash Version*. October 9. Accessed May 5, 2013. http://portal.wecreatestuff.com.

West, Joel. 2003. "How Open Is Open Enough? Melding Proprietary and Open Source Platform Strategies." Research Policy 32 (7): 1259–1285.

Winokur, Danny. 2011. "Flash to Focus on PC Browsing and Mobile Apps; Adobe to More Aggressively Contribute to HTML5." Adobe Blog. November 9. Accessed July 20, 2013. http://blogs.adobe.com/conversations/2011/11/flash-focus.html.

Wirman, Hanna. 2009. "On Productivity and Game Fandom." *Transformative Works and Cultures*. September 15. Accessed July 13, 2013. http://madisonian. net/2009/09/15/transformative-works-and-cultures-vol-3-2009.

Wood, Peter. 2003. "Everybody to the Limit." *National Review*. August 27. Accessed August 29, 2012. http://www.nationalreview.com/articles/207853/everybody -limit/peter-wood.

Worth, Stephen W. 1997. "Spumco's Web Cartoon Series Premiere!" Alt.animation. spumco. http://groups.google.com/group/alt.animation.spumco/browse_thread/ thread/be4d927b4cf1481c/8b7a601071fac610#8b7a601071fac610.

Wortham, Jenna. 2011. "Game that Critiques Apple Vanishes from App Store." *New York Times*. September 13. Accessed June 19, 2013. http://bits.blogs.nytimes. com/2011/09/13/game-that-critiques-apple-vanishes-from-app-store.

Young-Hae Chang Heavy Industries. 2000. *Bust Down the Door Again! Gates of Hell-Victoria Version*. Seoul: Flash.

Zickuhr, Kathryn, and Aaron Amith. 2013. "Home Broadband 2013." Pew Internet. August 26. Accessed September 9, 2013. http://pewinternet.org/Reports/2013/ Broadband.aspx.

Zuern, John. 2003. "Matter of Time: Towards a Materialist Semiotics of Web Animation." *Dichtung Digital*. February 14. Accessed August 5, 2012. http://www .dichtung-digital.de/2003/issue/1/zuern/index.htm.

Index